CORPORATIZED, MANAGED HEALTHCARE:

YOUR HEALTH - YOUR CHOICES - YOUR DISTRESS - MY DISMAY

By
Martin S. Finkelstein, MD, FACP

Library of Congress Control Number: 2025931695

Dedicated to all of Today's and Tomorrow's Doctors

Computers manage diseases and finances.....

Doctors treat patients

Good doctors treat diseases-

Great doctors treat patients with diseases

William Osler

Who among us passes through this life without needing Healthcare?

The secret in successfully caring for patients is to begin by caring for patients

HYMAN M. FINKELSTEIN, MD

TABLE OF CONTENTS

CHAPTERS

1 - BEING A PATIENT IN TODAY'S CORPORATE MEDICAL WORLD 3

2 - CHOOSING YOUR HEALTH INSURANCE 21

3 - CHOOSING AND INTERACTING WITH YOUR MEDICAL TEAM 51

4 - VALUE AND SIGNIFICANCE OF TESTING 75

5 - UNDERSTANDING MEDICATIONS 87

6 - CHOICES DURING EMERGENCIES 101

7 - SURVIVING HOSPITALIZATION 109

8 - HOME CARE 123

9 - STRUGGLING WITH END-OF-LIFE DECISIONS 129

10 - CHOICES IN PREVENTIVE CARE AND EARLY DETECTION 135

11 - CARE OF THE DISABLED 147

12 - PROTECTING YOUR HUMANITY 151

ACKNOWLEDGEMENTS 165

ABOUT THE AUTHOR 167

Preface

We are transitioning from personalized healthcare to corporate, managed healthcare in the United States. We all have witnessed great advances in the science of healthcare, but have paid a steep price in the human aspects of care delivered to the patient. The changes affect all patients in every component of their care, from office visits to emergency care. Testing is over-emphasized and overly ordered. Doctors are now employees of larger organizations whose decisions and work schedules are mandated by the organization. They have lost their autonomy. Selecting your health insurance is, at best, confusing and fraught with anxiety. Finding a family doctor who advises, counsels, explains, and supports the patient and the patient's family is now a rarity (and a luxury).

Computers and algorithms have greatly improved the quality of care to an average (or model patient) suffering from a model disease (a disease that follows an expected pattern). However, patients and diseases are never average in every respect and differ widely in their needs and responses. A computerized health record dictates the essentials of the visit by how it is programmed, focusing on the disease and complaint, and not on the patient as a unique complex individual.

We are becoming experts at managing diseases but need to improve our skills at managing patients. It is the patient who is seeking healthcare, not the disease. Private, profit-motivated companies have purchased many medically related facilities, increasing the debt these facilities must bear and reducing paid staff. Studies have shown a resulting decrease in performance quality. We now have health networks which restrict all care to non-subscribers. Together with health insurance, drug, and management companies, they dictate healthcare options through their decisions and threats to withhold payment for services they deny based on apparent costs. They are primarily motivated by profit and not by service or need. They negotiate for the lowest possible charges from any endorsed facility or medical group.

The consequences of these changes contribute to a healthcare system that is the world's most expensive (a multi trillion dollar industry), most complicated, and poorly satisfying to patients. Patients' control of, or influence on their healthcare has been lost, ceded to corporations, as many feel they are being manipulated.

Gaps in public health insurance encouraged private insurance companies to participate in healthcare. As a result, in addition to appealing to those not eligible for Medicare or Medicaid, private health insurance is actively trying to woo patients into switching their government health insurance to their private offerings called "Medicare Advantage." It tries to privatize all healthcare, offering many benefits not provided under public insurance. Patients should wonder, "Who is paying for all these added benefits? How can they afford all they promise?" The operating costs are staggering. In addition to paying for all the services they promise, costs include additional expenses for high executive salaries, salaries for the vast increase in the number of clerks and blue collar employees, their own liability insurance, actuaries, lawyers, dividends to shareholders, any interest on loans, expensive advertising, maintenance of corporate offices, and much, much more. Corporate healthcare is profit-motivated, not service-motivated. Healthcare costs increase dramatically with privatization.

The privatization of healthcare with corporate network control of the industry requires greater patient protection of their basic patient health needs. Our country urgently needs the creation of a National Health Authority that can oversee the healthcare industry in the US, protect consumers, and regulate corporations.

The Public has a right to be informed about the workings and machinations of an industry that so profoundly affects their health and lives. An informed public is the best protection we have against corporate abuse. It is my hope that this book will increase public awareness and provide further insight into our complex healthcare industry.

Chapter 1
BEING A PATIENT IN TODAY'S CORPORATE MEDICAL WORLD

In a system favoring uniformity, patients need to assert their individuality

Gone are the days of the beloved American TV doctors named James Kildare, Ben Casey, and Marcus Welby. These popular fictional doctors of the past represented paragons of compassionate generalists, who performed all medical procedures needed by their patients: from delivery of babies, to simple surgery, to healing the social and emotional difficulties they encountered in their practice. Their sole motivation was helping the patients under their care. They were considered extended members of the family: trusted and consulted for any family disturbances. These caring roles have been largely replaced with less personal and managed care as represented by responses such as "Not in Network," "Your Insurance is denied," "The next appointment is in 4 months."

US healthcare is currently in a transitional state, and significant, unwelcome consequences have come with the changes. Interacting with today's complex, multi-trillion-dollar healthcare bureaucracy, which comprises multiple diverse professions, services, and industries in the United States, is stressful at its best. Patients who don't recognize or understand this are accepting to be passive pawns, ripe for manipulation without being aware. They may be frustrated without understanding the cause of their frustration. We are rapidly transitioning from personalized healthcare into managed healthcare, or more accurately, corporate-managed healthcare. In this corporate healthcare world, profit and efficiency are the new priorities. Corporations control the money and thus dictate the policies. This holds for both private and government establishments. Businessmen and politicians with little to no education or experience in illness and disease have wrested the management of healthcare away from healthcare professionals. Issues that do not fit conveniently into the computer fields they composed hinder efficient management. The more unique and individual the patient's needs, the more significant will be the system disruption. In this context, patients having multiple distinctive personal issues threaten the system. Fitting complex human conditions of patients into preset computerized programs is like shoving square pegs into round holes. Patients are lumped together with others having some chosen similar problem. They are then treated as all others in this group. There will always be some strain, and patients often feel this strain.

Still, patient care is delivered one-to-one, involving only the patient and the caregiver (a doctor, nurse, or therapist). It is the outside control and regulation that has changed. To protect their own interests, patients must be more proactive and less passive while engaging with the healthcare industry today; more informed and less ignorant; more assertive of their humanity and less accepting of the hassles they encounter.

The readily accessible neighborhood family doctor is extinct. The doctor whom the patients historically entrusted with safeguarding their body, psyche, and health, the person to whom they confided their deepest secrets and candidly expressed their most personal problems, is gone. That supportive, deeply personal relationship has been replaced with one often bordering on being impersonal and mechanical—one based on algorithms and programmed computers. With the erosion of personalized medicine and motivated by profit and efficiency, we may soon find robots replacing doctors.

Healthcare today is so complicated that only a select few can understand its fine and fragmented details. Healthcare encompasses multiple professions and comprises many publicly and privately owned companies and governmental authorities (City, State, and Federal). They vie with each other for your business and market share. They incessantly bombard consumers through every available media with advertisements for their services and products to attract interest and enrollment. It's hard not to question their motivation. The average consumer is understandably confused, overwhelmed, and often annoyed by all the competing advertising for medical services, insurance, and medications. Consumers should not feel inferior for not understanding the offerings. Not understanding the details of the offerings is the rule and probably the intention.

Healthcare is a patchwork layering of contracted services that sometimes overlap and sometimes leave gaps in care. The big players are health insurance companies (health networks), insurance companies offering malpractice and other liability insurance, hospitals and other medical and health-related care facilities, medical groups that deliver healthcare, home care agencies, State and federal regulatory agencies, and Pharma (an entity representing pharmaceutical firms). Many new players are privately owned corporations that purchase health-related facilities and other corporations involved in healthcare. Together, they form a massive industrial complex with diverse components. It is becoming almost impossible for the consumer to know who owns and manages the health services they depend upon. Similarly, where does all the money that pays for their healthcare come from, and where is it going?

State governments set local state health policy, as demonstrated in how different states regard birth and death issues such as abortion, birth control, and physician-assisted suicide. States license doctors, all health providers, health facilities, and nursing agencies and regulate all health-related corporations. Without licenses and government permission, these corporations and individuals cannot legally operate. Governmental agencies monitor performance and adherence to their rules while reviewing all consumer complaints. With 50 different states, we have 50 different policies. But we are one nation, and people travel and relocate anywhere in the US at will. They are at risk of needing healthcare in a state other than their own and not knowing local health policies.

Each corporation involved in healthcare sets its internal policies (adhering to local government guidelines) and competes for market share. With endless mail, TV, and media advertising aimed at the consumer, the purpose seems to confuse them into questioning their prior medical decisions. These health-related industries employ skillful lobby groups to advance their positions with the government and protect their status quo. Somewhere, buried under this commanding, massive corporate network, are two small entities: the patient and the doctor. Despite being the industry's expressed focus, the bureaucracy makes both feel insignificant and powerless.

The medical landscape has changed considerably in the past century, as older individuals certainly recognize. Impressive advances in medical care are evident to everyone, with the development of new medications, new ways of testing, and new treatments. New diseases have appeared (e.g., Lyme Disease, COVID-19, post-traumatic stress, and new occupational and environmental toxic and infectious exposures). Populations have grown, and travel and mass migrations have brought increased mixing of diverse peoples, with closer contact among individuals having different health and social issues. In the more developed countries, people are surviving for decades with cancer, heart disease, kidney failure, and neurological diseases. Organ transplants of the liver, kidney, heart, or lung are almost commonplace. Life expectancy has increased by decades, leading to a more aged population with multiple chronic illnesses - diseases that, in the past, would have caused their death at a much younger age. They require more involved care. New problems don't arise in a vacuum. The more medications a patient takes, the more co-morbidities, the more internal scars and residuals of past diseases, the more complex the care that will be needed. And we expect the wonders of medical science and technology to continue and develop even more impressive cures and treatments.

As stated above, medicine in the US shed its image of the neighborhood family doctor who ran his solo practice only a few decades ago (few women went into medicine). The relationship between a doctor and his patient was very personal. With corporatization, the relationship has become less personal, with the attention of healthcare shifting away from the person and focusing more on the disorder. Doctor's autonomy has now essentially vanished. Medicine has become a massive corporate enterprise with enormous budgets and services. With changing needs and a more elderly and frail population, people need more medical and personal care than ever. Some might argue that essential medical care has not improved over what was delivered several decades ago, but none can say that it hasn't changed. It certainly costs a lot more. Availability and quality of medical care in the US are still spotty, depending on where a person lives, their wealth, ethnicity, and medical sophistication. However, with all our advances, we face challenges in delivering quality care to those in need. The changes in the delivery of this care can be confusing and frustrating to an older and more chronically ill population, who generally have more difficulty adapting to new realities.

American patients are routinely now met with such expressions as "Not in Network! Your Claim has been Denied! You Need Prior Approval! Your Co-Pay has Increased! We No Longer Accept Your Insurance! Your Insurance Coverage has Changed!" These responses demand a reassessment of the need and possibly a significant change in your care plan. But what do these statements require of the patient or caregiver? These determinations are made by the insurance carrier, who may change coverage at their discretion whenever they feel it would benefit the company. Should the subscriber switch health insurance to another company, adjust their medications, go to a different laboratory or facility, order different testing, or contest the denial decision? Your denial may have been based on a single improper coding number on a request for payment or services. (Code numbers exist for every patient, illness, service, location, and complication). The numbers keep growing in length and decimals as they require more and more digits to convey greater and greater requested details of the condition. Computer programs are fed code numbers, not words. The codes are needed to input all the "essential" data of the illness and treatment details into a computerized record. With all those numbers, mistakes occur and trigger a denial.

With today's increasing compartmentalization and complexity in healthcare, patients can be easily confused and not understand the reasons for decisions managing their healthcare.

These are new problems, and the traditional family doctor can no longer guide the patient. There is no longer the neighborhood independent family doctor who does everything and explains what is happening to the patient and the patient's family. Healthcare has become a vast industry that spends trillions of dollars annually and costs each American tens of thousands. Healthcare is a massive business now primarily aimed at making a profit and rewarding stockholders. The primary concern of the family doctor was the patient's health and welfare. The primary concern of private corporations managing the healthcare industry is profit and, often, greed. America has the world's highest healthcare cost, and all costs ultimately filter down to the taxpayer and consumer. Other countries have cheaper healthcare with greater public satisfaction.

Algorithms, programmed for an average patient with an expected response to an injury or disease, manage illnesses. This programming is critical to insurance payments and treatments as computers manage all aspects of the business. With computer involvement, improved care in the diagnosis and management of diseases has been impressive. Doctors can research information about diseases and approved treatments quickly on the Internet. However, this all pertains to managing diseases, not managing patients. Artificial intelligence (AI) and computer programs offer the potential for excellent disease care but not for patient care. Internet searches yield vast amounts of information and clinical results from multiple studies regarding any particular disorder but nothing about a single patient. Individual patients are hidden in the population like trees are lost in a forest. Clinical studies examine target populations, lumping diseased patients by some defined criteria, but individual patients are much more than their identified disease. Patients come with unique situations that differ widely. They are complex human beings with all the vagaries of being human. No two people have the same illness or react to medical or surgical emergencies in the same manner. Each person is unique in life and responds differently to disease or injury. There is no single care plan that fits all. People have different needs that need to be recognized. Good medical care is very personal. The treating doctor cares for a specific needy patient, not a population.

But, treating the disease and the patient cannot be separated. Every illness comes with many variable components affecting its outcome. Multiple variables (patient-related and disease-related) affect the patient and the illness. Regarding the patient, it is their past medical history, co-morbidities, lifestyle, hormonal status, age, gender, race, genetic makeup, medications taken, and unique social situations that strongly influence the risk of contracting an illness. Secondly, the illness often manifests itself differently regarding severity and symptoms in each person. Thirdly, the patient's ability to tolerate the prescribed treatment can influence the disease's progression and prognosis. Fourthly, how well the patient heals (which depends on their circulation, body defenses, etc.) and ability to follow the recommended treatment have a powerful effect. Other determinants include past smoking, occupational exposures, and behavioral factors. All these variables affect the outcome and complexity of care. No illness, injury, or disease exists independently of the patient. We notice these variables regularly when we see two people with the same diagnosis but very different disease severity and manifestations. Every sickness is like a complicated battlefield, with the patient fighting the disease and the disease fighting the patient. Adequate medical care swings the battle in favor of the patient, but sometimes, the disease still wins out. Why does one individual display little disturbance from the same disorder that hospitalizes another? It is not the diagnosis alone that determines the illness's outcome or impact. Medicine has no guarantees, and unrealistic expectations based solely on a diagnosis are doomed to disappoint.

Insurance company computers and Electronic Health Records (EHRs) cannot satisfactorily manage each patient's unique situation. They are programmed for what is expected and typical for the disorder based on prior experience with others. They create a model patient with a predicted way the disease will progress and how it should be treated.

With this model, companies can estimate needs and costs. Algorithms provide preprogrammed choices, and having a model patient and disease simplifies computer input. However, no one is the model patient, average in every aspect, and no disease is average. We can't expect everyone to react similarly to stress, illness, or injury. Not being average makes each patient something of a unique case, an outlier from the constructed model. How much of an outlier varies.

Take, for example, two patients, each with a diagnosis of diabetes and hypertension. The diagnosis is only a small part of the illnesses. It's the label, the name. It doesn't tell the whole story. The most crucial issues to the patient and the patient's family revolve around how sick and incapacitated the diseases have made the individuals and how the patients respond to treatment. There can be vast differences in how ill and functional the patients are. However, even with the same disease severity, it's how the disorders disturb their lives that matters the most to the patient. One individual may have an elderly bedridden relative living in their home who depends on the patient's assistance, while the other does not. One may be working full time, the other not. Treatment plans must consider all home conditions in their formulations. Discharging a patient from the hospital to their home where the situation is precarious or demands more of the patient than they can handle is inappropriate. These two patients cannot be treated and managed the same despite the same coded diagnosis and severity of illness. Many factors directly and indirectly influence how the same disorder can affect different people differently. Putting a label or code number on all these confounding variables is impossible. Human judgment and understanding is often required. Such judgment is not a computer-programmed entity at present.

Doctors today are encouraged to practice "Evidence-based Medicine." As its name implies, evidence-based care follows the guidelines and recommendations of well-conducted and researched studies that show the superiority of one treatment over another for any particular disease based on accepted evidence. Medical decisions are no longer grounded in the beliefs or intuitions of the treating provider but on documented published facts. Meta-analysis screening of all available pertinent studies by computer searches demonstrates the efficacy of the recommended treatment. Medical societies then support and publish these recommendations. This approach to medical care is a significant improvement in the way doctors treated diseases in the past. But once again, evidence-based medicine aims to treat diseases, not patients. It is the doctor, with the patient's consent, who must make the final choices, factoring in all the individual patient variables discussed above and observing how the patient responds. Their concern is the individual patient, not the model or average patient. Evidence-based medicine should be viewed as recommendations or guidelines and not as decrees.

Humans working in healthcare today are less involved in patient care than they had been in the past. Corporate regulations and computer operators have taken over many of their past managerial roles. Healthcare providers no longer have the independence and control of their practice that once existed. Healthcare workers don't have to think as much, as algorithmic programs do this for them. Patients and doctors should realize that algorithms are best employed to provide information for consideration, not as substitutes for thinking or clinical judgment. Computers have no brains. Perhaps, someday, this may be different, but presently, humans have the brains, and they should use them. When the algorithm is seemingly not dealing appropriately with a patient's deteriorating condition, the treating doctor has a responsibility to override the algorithmic recommendations and make an overriding decision. That's what patients expect, and that's the best therapy.

We live in a complex medical business world today. Your family doctor is no longer your "Virgil," who will guide you through the medical care and insurance maze, adding a human dimension to your care while understanding your particular difficulties. Computers, artificial intelligence, and algorithms have replaced humans in many functional ways. Patients, acting alone must now navigate an increasingly complex and bureaucratic healthcare system designed by corporate, government, and insurance executives. Few sick patients can manage this without help. And the sicker they are, the less capable they will likely be. Unless they have family support, those who are the most ill, those who are the most debilitated, those who are in greatest need of medical care are the ones who are expected to make their own medical decisions. Patients, as well as their doctors, are probably confused by all the new regulations.

In the past, neighborhood family physicians were more than just doctors. They were almost part of the family and could be relied upon for help, expert advice, and support. They understood their patient's physical, social, financial, and emotional difficulties and made suggestions based on a balance of all four. No outside agencies were controlling your care. And doctors were far more accessible. Indeed, there was no intermediary screening incoming calls or messages and running interference, who stood in the way of direct contact. Before making critical health-related decisions, patients unhesitatingly sought their doctor's opinion. Those days are now gone, along with the doctor's expected role. Indeed, many patients today can't even recall their doctor's name.

Proper medical care has always required a cooperative effort between the patient and the doctor. The patient is principal in this relationship and must fully participate in his or her care. After all, their body, family, and work will be affected by changes in their health. They should not be shy or afraid to offer their opinion or request further explanations from their caregiver. The relationship requires all parties to be honest, candid, and professional, with the sole objective being the patient's welfare. They are allies and should work together. If a patient doubts the need for any procedure, it should be discussed with the doctor. A patient cannot challenge or discuss anything with an algorithm. Financial concerns should not be paramount or replace the patient's life and welfare as the primary goal. Every patient should feel that their well-being is the principal concern of those caring for them. It is the patient's consent to the proffered care that is essential. They can accept or reject medical recommendations or switch providers, insurance carriers, or health facilities. It is this relationship that is being threatened.

Today, the family doctor is mainly replaced by medical group employees obligated to follow corporate regulations, guidelines, and insurance demands. Management decisions are made by some employee at the corporate headquarters, who never had any direct contact with the patient. Without a close doctor-patient relationship, patients are now forced to take more of the lead in their healthcare. For this, they need more education about the healthcare industry. Healthcare has become almost totally corporatized, and trying to reach a responsible human for help is not like it was in the past. Patients are not pawns to be moved about as inanimate objects, nor ciphers that computers and corporations can manipulate. Patients should not forfeit their primary role in their healthcare by relegating it to corporation clerks.

In business, time is money, and this extends to healthcare. Office visits must be scheduled way in advance. Rarely do patients experience the luxury of spending more than 30 minutes with their physician to query them about their medical concerns. More likely, they spend the bulk of their 10-15 minute visit with the medical assistant or nurse, and even then, they may feel too embarrassed to bring up any issues that are not immediately apparent or directly related to the chief complaint for which they are visiting the doctor. Phone contact with the doctor or medical assistant is often impossible as machines and computers with limited programmed or recorded responses answer phones. Patient portals on computers have replaced much of telephone communication. However, many people don't own a computer, and patient portals are not structured to facilitate questioning or personal dialogue. And, for the less computer-savvy and older patients, programmed portals are frustrating and challenging to navigate. Patients often need a human who understands their situation, can question them, understand what they are trying to say, and then direct them to the appropriate facilities. It's again the situation of a sick patient dealing with a complicated care system and bureaucracy. Trying to get simple healthcare advice, as was available only a few decades ago, has become an ordeal, if possible at all.

These issues are only getting worse. The doctor-patient relationship has fundamentally changed. Patients and their families or caregivers must become more sophisticated, proactive, and participatory in healthcare. They are asked to make decisions about unfamiliar issues. If they succeed in establishing contact with a purportedly medically sophisticated person, it is most often with an unknown stranger who offers assistance. It is someone who has never interacted with the patient and has not earned the consumer's trust. That unfamiliar person may give specific advice and suggestions, but can the patient trust this advice from a stranger as being appropriate? Are they trying to make a sale? Who is paying their salary? Do they have an ulterior agenda? Whomever you're talking to, are they experts at what they are advocating? Do they really understand the patient's concerns? Do they have access to your medical records? In the end, the patient must take some responsibility for their actions and make many of the decisions for which they had previously relied on the advice of their trusted family doctor. Understanding essential health and healthcare issues is vital and more important than ever.

Consider for a moment how you would react if, during some weekend evening, you experienced a new discomfort in your abdomen or side. In the past, if you had a trusted primary doctor whom you knew and respected, you would have called them for their advice. Your doctor might even have come to your home and made a house call to examine you. Not so at present. So, what are your current options? Should you call your primary care doctor anyway? Should you call a specialist, a gastroenterologist, or a rheumatologist? Should you go to an urgent care center or a local hospital Emergency Department? Should you call a family relative or friend who is more medically sophisticated than you? Or should you wait until Monday morning and try to reach your family doctor during regular office hours? The new discomfort might be something trivial and vanish quickly without any intervention, or it could be the first indication of something serious that requires urgent attention, as with the beginning of appendicitis, cholecystitis, or an arterial aneurysm. Going to a hospital or urgent care center will probably result in hours of waiting to be seen, assuming you found one open, and will your health insurance cover the medical services at that location? Will you be hospitalized for more observation, testing, or surgery? Or should you take an antacid and wait? How long should you wait to assess your status? What will you do? This is not a theoretical, unlikely scenario. It happens frequently and without warning - a new frightening complaint. Any randomly occurring event is four times more likely to occur "after hours," weekends, or holidays (40 weekly working hours out of 168 hours of the week - not even including in the calculation of any vacation or personal family time when your doctor is not readily available).

Calling your doctor's office can lead to a recorded message that states, "If this is an emergency, go to the nearest Emergency Department." That supposedly covers the doctor's responsibility for any problem and outcome. The expression is "covering your backside." And how, as a non-medical person, do you know if what you're experiencing is an emergency? You are being asked to diagnose your own condition. Suppose you are lucky enough to get a medically qualified person to answer the phone or call you back. In that case, it is likely someone who is not familiar with your medical history and someone not in the office. Does that individual have access to your health records? More likely, it will be someone who, by not knowing what is causing your discomfort, will recommend the Emergency Department option. That is the quickest and safest response that will protect the healthcare provider from a hefty lawsuit if the problem turns out to be serious. Unfortunately, no single, simple, and satisfactory answer to this scenario presently exists.

People will respond differently. Much depends on the level of anxiety and fear the symptoms engender. It depends on how severe the pain is, how it progresses, its character and changing nature, and how it affects you, the patient. The worse you feel and the more frightened you become, the more likely you will be to seek emergency attention. The erosion of the doctor-patient relationship makes this issue more problematic than it would have been decades ago. The consequences of any decision can be enormous in terms of health, finances, family, and social interactions. These are life-or-death issues and cause much anxiety and fear (not a time to make irrational decisions).

In today's healthcare world, the consumer is bombarded with television and mail advertisements promoting a particular competitive health insurance company, prescription medication, and even medical facility. Such advertising never existed several decades ago. The ads are frequently confusing, sometimes misleading, and only create greater anxiety and uncertainty in the consumer. They are intended to make consumers question whether they are taking the best medicines, have the wrong health insurance, or go to the wrong medical center. They commonly succeed in creating some uncertainty in your mind about your health status, and you may want additional advice and assurance from your health provider. Corporations spend a great deal of money on expensive marketing to woo you and get your business. They certainly don't know you, but they know how much money they will get if you choose their offering. Whose advice will the consumer seek when making their choices? Some ads end with "ask your doctor about …" But can you ask your doctor, medical assistant, or nurse practitioner, when your visit is short and time a valuable commodity? Frequently, your confusion revolves around costs and cost-effectiveness, which depends on many variables, including your underlying health, social situation, and finances. It's not a question of asking your doctor. It's a matter requiring a serious and more protracted discussion.

Although now virtually extinct, there still is a need and place for the primary care family doctor. If you can find one, consider yourself lucky. As discussed in subsequent chapters, primary care doctors are becoming scarce. They are undervalued and underpaid for their services. Despite their need, fewer graduating medical students seek careers in primary care. In this corporatized world, there is an increased need for patients to assert their humanity and insist on being treated as humans with medical needs and not as disorders.

There are several particularly worrisome or confusing common medical circumstances where patients seek assistance and advice from family, friends, and medical acquaintances. These include 1) Choosing the most appropriate health insurance for you and your family; 2) Selecting doctors, provider groups, and hospitals; deciding the need between specialty care or primary care for your particular health concerns; 3) Understanding the best way to take prescribed medications; 4) Knowing the purpose and value of recommended medical testing; 5) Preparing for medical emergencies; 6) Retaining your humanity and composure when hospitalized; 7) Appreciating the value of preventive care; 8) Getting the most out of your doctor's office visit; 9) Acquiring home care services.

Understanding the issues and problems involved with these challenges can help today's patients feel more confident in their healthcare decisions and better prepare them for any unexpected medical emergencies.

We all realize that healthcare restructuring through corporatization is the cause of these concerns. Corporatization changes everything and is a growing power that engulfs the existing health-related system. It brings benefits, opportunities, hardships, and challenges. It causes stress and anguish. But whatever we now complain about, this may be the best it gets. Things may get even worse.

Chapter 2
CHOOSING YOUR HEALTH INSURANCE

Policies change -The best choice today may not seem the best next year

With the staggering cost of healthcare, the need for health insurance is manifest. Providing healthcare today involves legions of individuals inputting and updating personal data, corporate executives deciding the extent of acceptable care, lawyers, and actuaries, aside from those who actually care for the patient. The vast bulk of health-related expenses is not destined for the providers who contact the patient directly and deliver personalized healthcare. Most of the costs go into paying the salaries of the legions of employees managing the involved businesses and corporations and into stock dividends. As stated above, the US has the most expensive and complicated healthcare worldwide. But even so, very few people anywhere on Earth can afford the cost of total comprehensive healthcare, and every government recognizes this need. Having health insurance provides some peace of mind. It allows a more relaxed night's sleep, not worrying if a sudden illness would strike and destroy your lifestyle with a pauperizing bill that will send your family into profound debt.

In the US, the creation of Medicare in 1965, insuring the elderly (over 65) for most of their healthcare expenses, was a watershed moment in our medical history. The elderly are the most vulnerable segment of our population because of their medical needs and costs. In a population essentially retired and with fixed income, they have the highest burden of health-related expenses. It was natural for the federal government to begin issuing health insurance for this population. Medicare was never designed to pay all of the health costs of its elderly subscribers. It was confusing and complicated from its very beginning. Medicare only covers 80% of the allowable amount they set (usually 10% less than their approved charge), and this 80% is paid only after an annual deductible. Medicare pays for only 90 consecutive days of hospitalization for any illness. However, patients have 60 lifetime reserve days to cover longer stays. There are different restrictions and limits on nursing home, psychiatric, and rehabilitation care.

Medicare is divided into Part A, which covers hospital and facility costs, and Part B, which covers provider or practitioner fees. Insurance costs for this Part B coverage are deducted from the subscriber's social security payments. Part A comes with no cost to the patient. Why were these "holes" in their coverage drafted into the original or traditional Medicare plan? Why did Medicare pick the age of 65 to offer health insurance? Why didn't Medicare choose to cover 100% of the costs and make it easier to understand? Why did they create the annual deductible and allocate 20% of the costs to the individual? It probably was to share some financial responsibility with the consumer and the necessity to get enough congressional approval to pass the legislation. Shouldn't those requiring and consuming medical care pay more than those healthy individuals who do not need medical care? Politicians make these decisions, and politicians always look at what would be politically acceptable to their constituents and what they could get passed in legislation. To some Americans, these financial gaps may not be a burden, but to most, they can significantly strain the family budget. It all depends on the individual's wealth and health. Medical debt is a major problem with many Americans. Too often, it competes with buying food or enjoying some luxury. This is particularly true for payments for hospitalizations, institutional care, and care for chronic illnesses like cancer, which can be astronomical. Common illnesses are a burden to some, but catastrophic illnesses are a nightmare to all.

And how did Medicare arrive at its payment schedule? Original fee schedules were set by legislators who probably wanted to set rates the medical profession would accept and consider "reasonable" but not extravagant. Since 1987, they have used a Sustainable Growth Rate to control spending and allow small increases in payments to allow for inflation, cost of living, and increased medical office costs. However, in 2013, under political pressure, they implemented a two percent reduction in payment fees to reduce government spending. Private insurance companies look to Medicare schedules as a guide for their payment schedules for services to their subscribers. Thus, federal decisions about Medicare affect everyone's insurance and the fees health professionals will be paid for their services. There are additional complexities if these Medicare details aren't confusing enough to the patient. Doctors can be Medicare accepting or non-accepting (non-accepting is discussed below). In the accepting category, doctors can be participating or non-participating). Participating doctors have agreed to accept Medicare's assigned and approved fee schedule, which is 95% of its allowable charges. Non-participating doctors can charge the patient more, and Medicare will pay 15% more for their allowed charges. Medicare publishes allowable and approved charges for every community and service, which they calculate annually. This confusing payment schedule is apparent to anyone getting a copy of their medical bill, which lists the amount billed, the amount allowed, the amount paid by insurance, and the amount that can be billed to the patient.

Although clearly stated in the plan, patients may not realize that Medicare Part B includes an annual deduction that the patient must pay before any Medicare payments begin. A yearly deduction is also included in private health insurance, although different plans offer different coverage. Each year starts anew. At the beginning of the year, doctors sometimes delay filing a claim, hoping another provider's bill will have fulfilled the patient's deductible. Also, Medicare has a limit on how many hospital days for any disorder they will insure, but do provide for "lifetime" days for which patient's bills will get paid. These lifetime days are not renewable. Medicare payments stop when all lifetime days (currently 60 days) are exhausted. Medicare rules are determined by Congress, which can change any Medicare features they wish and can pass. For example, Medicare now pays for younger patients with chronic kidney disease needing dialysis and those with ALS (Lou Gehrig's disease). Patients are usually, and understandably confused about insurance costs and payments. They should not feel embarrassed or bad for not understanding the insurance details they purchased or were provided. Most people, including providers, are similarly confused. The terminology is puzzling: participating, nonparticipating, allowable, approved, actual, residual, deductible, and accepting. It's far too complicated. Tomes or volumes are needed to explain all the conditions that regulate Medicare and other health insurance. It's far too complex for the average patient or provider to understand. Hospitals and health group facilities have employed trained specialists to handle their insurance disagreements and coding. Improper coding can cost the facility considerable amounts of revenue. Other groups outsource these services to billing firms. Doctors in solo practice will have great difficulty. We, in America, can probably boast of having the most expensive healthcare system in the world and the most confusing and complicated system to boot.

By leaving gaps in their health insurance coverage, Medicare opened the door for private insurance companies to partner in the public domain of Medicare by offering supplemental, or gap insurance.. But, private health insurance is needed for all

Americans under 65 and those without public health insurance. New health insurance companies sprung up to fill this need. Before the creation of Medicare, Blue Cross/Blue Shield was the only substantial health insurance in the country. It expanded in the 1950s to address the growing public demand for health insurance coverage, but competition increased rapidly after Medicare demonstrated the necessity of having health insurance. Employers are pressured to purchase private health insurance for their employees. The cost of such insurance varies directly with the benefits offered. Not all employee insurance benefits are the same, and if the employer is trying to save money, the plan and benefits purchased may shock the employee when they receive their first medical bill. Subscribers should read and understand the benefits of the policy they are offered. They may wish to pay more out of pocket for more comprehensive insurance. Those without employment health benefits can purchase group insurance (if in a recognized group) or as individuals. Costs vary by the conditions covered and how large a group is insured. It is expensive insurance and takes its lead from Medicare, adjusting its payments using Medicare as its guide (including deductions and fees). Patients are usually interested in something other than the details of charges and expenses. They simply want to know how much they must pay for any needed medical services. This vital aspect is usually challenging to estimate and can be shocking when patients learn the full details.

Patients should be aware of the continued pressure on private insurance companies and facilities to increase profits by whatever means they can, including negotiating for cheaper services and increasing premium revenues. Public health services also are trying to reduce their costs. Changes in premiums and fees are corporate decisions that may suddenly be sprung on the consumer and provider at any time. For consumers, whichever insurance they think is best today may not be the best for them tomorrow.

Unfortunately, most insurance plans cannot be switched by the consumer until a "window" for enrollment or change opens. Corporate decisions control healthcare. If you are worried or confused, it is best to ask your insurance carrier for any specifics regarding your coverage, as your medical providers will probably not know the answer.

Most of the population is not over 65 and does not qualify for Medicare. For the more indigent, each state in the US developed its version of Medicaid, which provides free health insurance for the unemployed or those unable to afford basic insurance costs. Medicaid also pays for home attendants and many other services not covered by Medicare. A needs assessment is required before Medicaid is obtainable. Many elderly fall into a hole when their health costs increase to an amount they cannot afford. Their income from social security or pensions may place them in the category of not being eligible for Medicaid, but their medical expenses exhaust their monthly income. Medicaid has a spend-down component. If, in paying their health-related bills, the residual income brings the individual into an adjusted income level that meets the Medicaid acceptance threshold, Medicaid assistance can be offered. It will pay for medical expenses above this threshold. Other insurance may have a "doughnut" provision, which pays an initial amount (after any annual deduction), followed by an amount not covered until this non-payment "hole" is paid by the consumer, and then better coverage begins again. Some insurance offers catastrophic coverage, when the financial burden is "catastrophic" or beyond the means of nearly everyone.

Needing Medicaid assistance is common when older people enter nursing homes and where the ongoing custodial charges of institutional care place the patient into the needs category. However, most Americans living at home do not qualify for Medicaid or Medicare and have average medical expenses. This population has the most to worry about. The wealthy can afford their average medical costs, and the indigent rely on Medicaid to pay theirs. Those in the middle are faced with the problem. They may find purchasing health insurance as an individual is too expensive and unnecessary. They feel well, have never had a severe illness, and hope they will never need costly healthcare. The Affordable Health Care Act of 2010 (ACA or Obamacare) sought to make healthcare more affordable for all Americans. It eliminated the existence of pre-existing conditions as an excuse for not offering health insurance or making premiums excessively high for individuals with chronic illnesses. It made purchasing private health insurance available and affordable for most Americans. It extended coverage to individuals under 26 previously insured under their parents' family plan. It provided subsidies to states that accepted the federal conditions and expanded Medicaid availability to poorer Americans.

It should be noted that the ACA does not require businesses to provide health benefits to their workers - it is optional. Trade unions, public pressure, and the need to attract more employees encourage employers to purchase such insurance. State and local authorities can help employers acquire insurance, including family plans. The situation often arises in families when both employed adults have family plan health insurance coverage as an employee benefit. It seems like a duplication of insurance with double the costs and benefits. The families will need to work out their situation and may choose to drop one of the plans whose benefits appear less favorable than the other. Insurance companies will not double pay for any healthcare. They will ask or choose which insurance is primary and which is secondary. They are very good at controlling their expenditures. The insurance purchased by the employer may not be the best or adequate to meet the employee's needs, and employees may have to make some difficult decisions about how much they can afford to pay for added benefits. Health insurance protection for the employee will eventually stop if the employment stops. Fortunately, if this happens, COBRA coverage allows the individual to stay on their job-based plan for a specified time (usually 18 months) while they try to get new insurance. However, many Americans still have healthcare insecurity, as they cannot afford their insurance premiums if they become unemployed and lose their income. They could apply for Medicaid if their needs increase, and resources fall below the threshold set for Medicaid acceptance. This leaves a time gap of uncertainty and healthcare vulnerability. Medicaid also sets more restrictive limits on payments for care, which would be paid only to those facilities approved by and accepting the lower fee schedule of Medicaid.

By setting the provider fees for health professionals, Medicare (and by extension all private health insurance) needed to create a value system for healthcare - a system which would determine the compensation for the delivery of healthcare fairly and appropriately. Marketplace economics was no longer operating. How much value should be approved for a particular surgery, therapy, procedure, or office visit? How much should the value be adjusted according to the location, the provider's credentials or experience? Should the prestige or community service of the providing facility affect its just compensation? How much should the compensation be adjusted according to the operating costs of the provider? How much should the complexity or time needed for the service be figured into the financial determination? The government tried to develop a fair payment system. How could the complexity of the patient's status be included in the calculus? There are so many variables concerning the provider, the patient, the issue, and the treatment in regard to severity and complexity that had to be put into the computer formulations for fair compensation. Code numbers needed to be created for all the possibilities and variables. And so, to create a system that tried to compensate providers in a more appropriate way for such complexity, modifiers were needed. Modifiers allowed for ancillary information about the complexity of care needed during a visit. Modifiers would address further issues that made the service.more difficult or complex and which would therefore justify greater compensation. Modifiers added a further dimension to the coding. All these variables make reasonable payments extraordinarily complex and critical. This complex coding determined the provider's income. Billing experts were needed, but their salaries and expenses were not paid by the insurance. The days of the solo primary generalist or family doctor ended. Doctors could easily spend more of their time with paperwork, computer inputting, and coding than in caring for patients. Even with the expanded coding system that was created, many of the less common variables were not even considered. Complaints and conflicts were certain to occur when any of the participating parties felt they were not being treated or compensated fairly. Some consequences of this payment system are discussed in the following sections.

The Veterans Administration provides free comprehensive healthcare to all veterans in their network of Veterans hospitals. However, the Veterans healthcare system is vulnerable to congressional legislation, and complaints of inadequate funding are frequent. Then there is the Indian Health Service, which is intended to provide comprehensive free healthcare to Native Americans. However, it, too, is underfunded, and medical facilities are located in sites poorly accessible to many Native Americans who do not live on reservations .In the United States, we have large numbers of visitors, migrant workers, and new immigrants who may require medical attention while here but lack any US insurance. Many people around the world are hesitant to travel to

America in fear of becoming ill, having no insurance, and getting hefty medical bills. Hospitals cannot deny care to those in need, but the bill will go unpaid if the individual has no medical insurance coverage or the means to pay the bill.

Then there is the Federal Employees Health Benefit plan (FEHB) which offers members of congress excellent health insurance options at low cost. This is a publicly managed health plan with excellent retirement and active health insurance policy choices which are heavily subsidized by the government (members pay 30% of its cost).

Workers Compensation insurance is required in most states for businesses having employees. This private insurance is paid by the employer and offers cash benefits to those workers unable to work, along with paying for any needed medical or surgical care for those who are injured or become ill as a result of their job.

Despite the cost and good intentions of our healthcare system, many Americans fear losing their health insurance and not being able to get the needed healthcare they desire. Americans pay the most for healthcare but are not the most satisfied with the care they get. To reiterate: Medicare (A and B) is federal health insurance, and Medicaid is a state government insurance plan for poorer residents. Aside from health care in the military, in prisons, and in other government agencies, all other health insurance is private. Private insurance companies can be divided into profit and nonprofit entities. Not-for-profit health insurance or health facilities (hospitals) do not pay profit dividends to their investors, may pay lower taxes, and are not as profit-motivated as their profit-driven counterparts. But they must remain fiscally solvent (including payment for executive salaries, which they determine) or go bankrupt. Many hospitals have closed due to bankruptcy. For-profit private insurance companies and facilities are motivated by profit (as the name implies) and sometimes by greed. They are not supported by charitable donations and are taxed for their earnings. They pay dividends to their shareholders. Many private insurance companies actively compete to get subscribers to their health plans. Private equity firms seek to purchase medical facilities (discussed below).

With the rising cost of pharmaceuticals, the government added a non-mandatory need to purchase "credible" drug insurance, or Medicare Part D, for their Medicare subscribers. Although labeled as Medicare insurance, it is privately managed. Currently, Medicare does contribute 11% of its budget to offset the cost of medications. The health insurance companies rushed in to fill this need. Many insurance plans are available for pharmaceutical insurance, each with multiple choices that differ in their premiums, deductibles, copays, and medications they cover. Tier 1 pharmaceuticals are usually generic, are older drugs, and are the cheapest. Drugs in Tier 3 are newer and more expensive; they may require prior approval before the company pays anything. There is always a copay, which varies according to the tier. Pharmacists can spend frustrating hours on the telephone checking patients' drug coverage and eligibility. Starting in 2025, there is an annual "cap" on medication costs for Medicare-covered patients. The public should be informed that Medicare A, B, and D require the individual to be enrolled as soon as their age allows (age 65). Delaying Medicare enrollment to a time when a new health need demands purchasing insurance brings a stiff penalty. The income derived from healthier subscribers subsidizes the expenses of the more needy ones. That is an insurance axiom. Waiting for the need to buy the insurance is a poor option that does not save funds.

I'm sure many Americans who feel healthy, invincible, and never get sick question the need for health insurance. If they had a choice, they would not purchase it. This is wishful, simplistic thinking and naivete on their part. It's also selfish thinking. They may resent paying for the healthcare of fellow Americans who require expensive care. It's understandable. But their time will come when they will have the need. They accept that they must purchase automobile insurance if they want a car. They need home insurance if they want to own a house or apartment. Some insurance is required - and health insurance is one of these. After an accident or the onset of an acute illness, these individuals can arrive at a hospital emergency room and demand health care that cannot be denied. But they never paid for it. And if they can't afford the care, we all will pay. They will be billed and may become financially insecure. They are putting themselves and their family into an economically vulnerable position.

There are obligations to living in a society. If people are unhappy with these obligatory costs, they can complain to their government representatives at the voting booth. Or they can move to another society in another country where everyone is covered with national healthcare, and their taxes will pay for it.

An obstacle to purchasing health insurance is the complexity and confusion of choices. The process of subscribing can be prohibitive. Many insurance companies recognize this and retain employees who assist in purchasing insurance. Even with this help, the choices and decisions are still too cumbersome and frightening for many elderly people who enlist the aid of their families. These are important decisions, and the uncertainties of future needs make the choices difficult.

The time to purchase insurance is before calamities happen. And we all know that illnesses occur without warning. They will come. And they come with a price tag sometimes a hefty price tag. Accidents happen in an instant and may require surgery and expensive, prolonged rehabilitative care. Those who feel they are healthy and immortal are deluding themselves. We know there is only one alternative to growing old and acquiring a greater cumulative risk of contracting diseases (acute and chronic). Most of us do not want to consider or accept that alternative. However, many still need help to afford the high insurance costs. Health insurance is not cheap. Each insurance carrier offers various plans, differing in premiums and offering different benefits with more choices to be made by the confused subscriber. After struggling to pay the high insurance premiums for years, many patients expect all their medical expenses will be covered and they should be entitled to premier service. They might only recall some of the policy details they chose and appreciate the full impact of their decision only after the bills arrive. When purchasing the insurance, the conditions listed are in the abstract, but when making a claim, they become a reality. Other patients argue that their out-of-pocket payments are much less than the cost of additional private insurance coverage and that purchasing insurance is not worth the expense. Paying for healthcare is a serious problem. We all recognize the problem, but the best solution still evades us.

However, there was another problem with the Medicare system. Congress sets the annual budget for Medicare. They calculate the amount budgeted by prior years' needs. This is done by guesswork and estimation, which leaves great uncertainty. What if an unanticipated medical problem hit the country (as happened with COVID-19 - although the government needed to step in with new legislation to cover the immense financial burden)? Was the Medicare system prepared, and could it accept such risk? Could Congress respond quickly enough to avoid a disaster? Private insurance companies argued they would assume the risk if given adequate government (tax-payer) funds. That way, Medicare and the government would know beforehand their annual expenses and could plan and budget for that amount: no surprising costs and no financial risk. Insurance companies know how to deal with risks, not governments. Medicare agreed to subsidize private insurance by 26% of its budget. It sounded simple.

Adopting this offer spawned the creation of Medicare Part C or Medicare Advantage Plans. If given enough federal money, they could cover drugs, dental, eye care, hearing, and all medically-related costs, including the funds allocated for annual Medicare B premiums from social security. They would cover whatever the government or their subscribers desired if they received enough funding upfront. Indeed, some plans offer help with rent, groceries, and other essential needs. It is no longer straightforward health insurance. Companies expand to help subsidize services and commodities that the average consumer requires. This inflated form of insurance could easily be reconfigured as comprehensive medical insurance, but it is not governmental nor universal. Despite having "Medicare" in its name, it is **not** Medicare and may not be an "Advantage" to the consumer. It is a private comprehensive medical insurance run for profit, but all American taxpayers pay a big part of the cost. More importantly, it is only accepted by some providers and services. And it is competitive, with many competing companies offering such comprehensive insurance (suggesting it is very profitable). Where is the public oversight to ensure the companies are meeting their responsibilities?

Moreover, the formation of Medicare Advantage plans opened a pathway for private health insurance companies to attract older patients, luring them away from their federally managed Medicare insurance. It is a step towards privatizing Medicare by offering Medicare in more attractive wrappings. Many Medicare Advantage plans are particularly targeting individuals covered by both Medicare and Medicaid. They are tempting such patients to exchange both their federal and state health insurance for the private insurance they offer. They tell the consumer how many more benefits they will get for "free" by switching. But at what future risk? With government insurance, there is government oversight and control. As private insurance, the control shifts to businessmen making corporate decisions. Many politicians in America have sought to abolish Medicare since its inception, viewing government involvement in healthcare as socialism, a challenge to American capitalism. Medicare Advantage fits nicely into their agenda. However, since this insurance requires support from the government, it is always at risk of losing support by congressional (? or executive) decisions. Insurance companies have no control over governmental decisions. They may have influence (as with lobbying) but no control. If insurance companies lose federal support, how will their subscribers be affected, and how high will their premiums rise?

Patients often ask whether they should get Medicare Advantage. But remember, private insurance requires profit, so when asked where they thought the additional funding to pay for all the enticing additional benefits came from, these individuals looked puzzled. It comes from all taxpayers. We're all paying for it: we and the subscribers.

However, the private insurance companies were not content with getting additional government funds. They wanted increased profit by decreasing their expenses. So, they began negotiating to get cheaper services. They do this for all the services their policies insure. They grow their income with higher subscriber fees and increased federal funds. They also decrease their expenses by bargaining for lower fee schedules, which makes some services and procedures more difficult to obtain. For providers, accepting the lower fee schedule does not preclude the insurance company from returning to doctors and facilities the following year and offering an even lower fee schedule. The private insurance company aims to get the lowest payments for their subscriber's care. Although they must pay the contracted amount for health-related services, they can attempt to renegotiate lower payments through contract renewals.

Consequently, many providers refuse to accept patients with Medicare Advantage insurance. This relates to physicians, laboratories, radiological services, etc. This is why the plans often state they have “a large network of providers.” Subscribers must use the services in that network. However, their network may not include your chosen physician and care at your preferred facilities. You must investigate these concerns before enrolling in Medicare C. Moreover, since facilities and insurance coverage can change at any time, your decisions may not be to your satisfaction next year.

Medicare fee schedules are not negotiated; they are set by policy. Many providers may consider them insufficient, but unlike private health insurance, Medicare does not threaten to withdraw payments if providers and facilities do not accept their fee schedule. This is a significant difference between government and private health insurance, and the consequences can be dramatic. Government may be inefficient and too political, but it is not motivated by profit and greed.

To protect the vulnerable public from unscrupulous charlatans or dishonest doctors who provide patients or insurance companies with fraudulent or inflated charges, the government felt regulations and oversight were needed. To ensure providers were providing appropriate care, the government required regular and timely educational updates and competency examinations. Forms and explanations were demanded. Insurance companies (public and private) with the access to patient's EHRs that are built into the programs, can seek explanation and justification for the provider's orders and procedures. With these tools, government or private insurance companies can function as a "big brother," watching the way every provider is treating their patient. They can then grade the performance of every provider around the country in how quickly and effectively they managed any particular disease, and how much it cost the insurance company. All charges come into their computer systems and they keep the records. They can then compare the behavior of any provider with the national or regional norm for any disease or procedure. They can tell when providers are not performing well or up to standard. They have all the pertinent patient data and medical/surgical data to work with. But again, they are looking at average patients and average diseases that fit into the computer programs. They may not see the patient in the same way the provider does. Their analysis may be flawed. While the justification for these practices is clear, they also impose additional demands on a providers valuable time: non rewarded time that would need to be taken from family or patient time. Overregulation is a serious complaint of the regulated. It has its negative impact on provider satisfaction.

All insurance payments (private and government) are determined by the service code, reflecting the nature of the office visit, and adjusted by the time and complexity involved. No adjustments are made to the doctor's or healthcare worker's experience or expertise. By their policy, a doctor is a doctor, period. A doctor who has been in practice for six months gets the same insurance payment as one with 20 or 30 years of experience. In groups where the group does the billing and funding, the disbursement of income is controlled by the group. The group can disperse collected funds any way they choose, usually with a lower salary and requiring more night, weekend, and holiday coverage to new members than to established ones.

The term "prior approval" was coined by private insurance companies. This is another way for these companies to control expenses. Prior approval for referrals, costly tests, procedures, and pricey medications became common. This approval is required before the insurance company will dispense any funds. And who approves or rejects giving such consent for the requested prior approval at the insurance company? A secretary, an office clerk, a nurse, a doctor, or a computer with an algorithm? The longer the insurance company can delay or withhold payment, the longer the funds remain with the company, earning interest. One or two months of this retained capital will amount to considerable money for the insurance company.

Whoever makes payment determinations undoubtedly never saw the patient and never reviewed all their medical data. An unknown and nameless stranger decides to grant approval and pay for the prescribed services or products based on a limited set of data they are provided and an algorithm generated by the insurance company. Often it is an employed nurse who makes these decisions, but it can also be someone who never had any significant hands-on or real-time experience caring for any sick, frightened, or handicapped patient. The denial of approval tells the patient their insurance will not pay for the recommended medicine or surgery. Although the insurance company may claim they are not practicing medicine or surgery, their denial has this effect. Who knows your medical situation better - your doctor or the insurance clerk? Without adequate explanation, denial of payment implies the doctor's orders were inappropriate; therefore, the insurance is not obliged to pay the bill. Insurance companies have no license nor authority to practice medicine, but their actions belie this. Suppose the insurance company disapproves of the requested medication or procedure. In that case, the patient and doctor are left with few options: challenge the denial, choose another treatment or procedure the insurance company would approve, require the patient to pay the total cost of treatment, or wait and switch to another insurance company when the window for selecting insurance next opens. Challenging the denial will require much telephone time, filing reports, and sending requested documentation from the doctor. Time and effort taken from other patients, and without any monetary compensation or "billable hours.". The denial does not come with a satisfactory explanation for their decision making contesting the decision more burdensome. In an appeal, the worst thing that can happen to the insurance company is that they would eventually have to pay for the service or medicine without any penalty or interest for their delayed determination. In the interim, the patient is not receiving the treatment ordered. It is the patient who suffers. The actual reason for rejecting claims is usually that the provider of services had not agreed to accept the reduced fees demanded by the insurance company. These fees are lower than those permitted by Medicare. These denials also serve as a veiled warning to providers who are undecided about accepting or rejecting the insurance conditions.

The selling point of health insurance carriers is their number of subscribers. The greater the number, the greater the clout the company enjoys. Offering their endorsement of a facility or provider is backed by the potential gain (or loss) of their subscribers as patients. Insurance companies solicit services at negotiated lower costs from laboratories, radiology, and medical care facilities in return for additional referrals. Most private health facilities and doctors refused to lower their standard charges, and it became challenging for doctors 'offices to find referrals for patients with Medicare Advantage. However, large facilities and groups usually feel it necessary to accept such patients as the number of potential patients grows. It's a business decision. Insurance carriers now flood the networks with advertisements for their version of Medicare Advantage. They depend on attracting an increasing number of subscribers. Their marketing includes pictures of an official Medicare card, in red, white, and blue, with "Medicare" boldly displayed on the front. In a very small font type, it mentions Medicare Part C is "not associated with any government agency." The amount of effort and money spent on advertising emphasizes how lucrative Medicare Advantage must be. It encourages Medicare patients to switch their health insurance from a nonprofit federal health plan to a profit-motivated private one. The consumer must realize that despite including the word "Medicare" in Medicare Advantage, such insurance is profit-motivated, not a public service. Each health insurance company seems to be marketing its version of Medicare Part C.

Each Medicare Advantage plan requests the subscriber's zip code to check eligibility for all the features they will offer. Individuals with Medicaid or limited financial resources may benefit and qualify for added services. But why is a zip code required to judge eligibility rather than having a needs assessment as is common with Medicaid? Why should the home zip code be instrumental in determining a patient's need? The answer to all these questions of why private health insurance places restrictions on their plans is always anticipated corporate "profit" and ease of administration. Rather than having a subscriber-income-based fee schedule, which would need costly investment in investigating each subscriber's financial status, they chose a geographic indicator for their expected profits in regional communities. It's cheaper and more straightforward. What these plans offer in their coverage and what they will charge subscribers is not based on the individual's healthcare needs nor capacity to pay, but instead on where they live. This is yet another example of the healthcare industry ignoring the human aspects of the individual in favor of treating subscribers as items, dots on a map. It focuses on the patient's neighborhood and residence (which are defined) instead of on the individual (who is more complicated). Health insurance companies have all the personal demographic data and statistics to adjust their policies and offerings to achieve their greatest projected profit.

Privatizing healthcare comes with huge increases in costs not encountered with public healthcare: competitive executive salaries; increased clerical staff; costs for the additional offered services; advertising and marketing; legal services, loan debt and interest payment; shareholder dividends; and probably much more. The paramount need for corporate profit is not there with public health services. But privatization comes with some significant advantages: a competitive marketplace with the ability to change policies and products without political infighting and control.

Patients who prefer to choose their providers and facilities of service may choose something other than an advantage plan. Those who frequent clinics or walk-in urgent care centers may find advantage plans genuinely advantageous. Extensive marketing is not cheap and only adds to the company's need to increase its profits to cover the added expenses. Medicare Advantage is an advantage only if the subscriber is content with using the medical facilities that accept this insurance and whether they will be satisfied with the care at that facility. There is a risk involved. Many Americans find that their preferred medical facilities will accept Medicare Part C. To them, subscribing to the Advantage program is rewarding and more affordable. But it's the insurance company that's making all the decisions. They can add or discontinue participation with any physician or facility at their discretion, leaving the patient scrambling to find another provider.

This is not to say that Medicare Advantage is a hoax, scam, or not worth purchasing. It can provide comprehensive coverage at a cheaper rate than the patient may currently have. It depends on continued governmental subsidy at a high level and the availability of facilities and providers that accept the lower fee schedules.

Neither of these variables is fixed or certain and may change at any time. The consumer should read the contract carefully and understand all its pros and cons as well as potential risks. The government is not going to disappear and has a strong economic debt rating - not so with private corporations.

As stated above, even without Medicare Part C, private medical insurance networks try to negotiate lower fee schedules in return for approving medical care at that facility. Health Insurance carriers compete to enroll practitioners and facilities into their network. They are better organized than care providers and have a stronger position in bargaining and negotiations. When facilities or physicians state "not in network" or "not covered," what are they saying? Why are they not in the insurance network, or are the services not covered? Is it because the insurance company demands too great a discount on the charges? Can the parties not agree on a fair or acceptable fee schedule? Does another competing insurance company restrict access to patients by some contractual agreement? These restrictions are imposed because of business and payment decisions, and the patient is the one who suffers as a result. The patient is the pawn being manipulated in this conflict. They may not be able to see the provider they prefer or get the care at the facility they want. They don't want to hear a receptionist tell them, "Your insurance has declined the bill," after getting the service. The current system hurts the patient. It does not improve healthcare.

Another separate kind of health insurance is long-term health insurance. This optional insurance is not cheap and is purchased from other insurance carriers. It pays for home care, nursing care, and home medical equipment. It may even provide some income when disabled after other insurance payments expire. Different policies are offered depending upon the definition of "disabled," the period an individual has to be disabled before benefits commence, and what the benefits will be. The premiums charged are directly related to the benefits offered.

Unifying and simplifying our healthcare and having a National Comprehensive Health system for all Americans is still an issue for this country. Health insurance purchased must be accepted throughout the country at the very least. Traveling or visiting a relative in another US state or area should not result in losing insurance coverage. We accept the reality of not having health insurance if traveling abroad, but this would be helpful. Most other developed countries have national health insurance which covers all residents. You pay taxes, and you get health care coverage. Easy, simple, and understandable. Being a foreign visitor to those countries usually comes with gratuitously needed healthcare, which their government covers. However, we do not reciprocate with gratuitous healthcare in the US, which a corporation must cover.

Proposals for expanding Medicare to all in the US, without age or need restrictions, or creating a new system entirely, are repeatedly suggested. The wish for a single payer system would simplify much of our services, reduce patient anxiety, and save much revenue. Such plans are, as expected, vigorously opposed by private health insurance companies and private facilities. Private health insurance companies spend a lot of subscriber money lobbying Congress to maintain the status quo regarding healthcare payments. How much of our annual healthcare expenditures could be reduced if we adopted a more straightforward, simpler system that eliminates the bulk of employees now needed to regulate and navigate the complexity of healthcare that now exists? Consumers might even be able to understand their insurance.

Paying for healthcare is more than just a local and national problem. No country can afford to provide comprehensive and total healthcare for all its residents (or "everything for everyone").

This reality is universally recognized, but the dilemma is to choose what disorders or costs will be covered by insurance. Furthermore, who will make these critical decisions and who will be insured becomes an issue. Rationing healthcare and setting limits are necessary.

Every society's current dilemma is how to ration health care fairly, compassionately, and justly. These are not medical decisions; they are societal.

1) Should the patient's age determine the availability of expensive care? This policy would require that no one over a defined age should get expensive care since their life expectancy was statistically limited. The question would be to decide the age to cut off medical payments for any particular condition, and how expensive is expensive? For this reason, dialysis for the elderly was once not an option in Great Britain.

2) Should the cost-effectiveness of the treatment determine the option? This may sound simple, but cost-effectiveness requires judgmental decisions on value for the money. But how does one define value? And value to whom: society, the family, the patient? Is treating a prisoner or unemployed vagrant less valuable than treating an older corporate executive or congressman? Is any person's life more valuable than another's, and who makes that determination? Cost-effectiveness brings apparent problems. Families of dying patients often demand "everything be done" to keep their loved one alive. This is understandable but usually futile, forces the patient to suffer longer, and is very expensive for a few more hours or days of hospital life. Should therapy be denied?

3) Should rationing be decided by the nature of the test or treatment availability? Limiting the availability or access to required equipment or procedures would result in long delays

for such services. Many individuals living in countries with a National Health plan complain of the long waits they must endure to get requested care. The longer the delay and wait, the less likely it would be needed (the patient might die, move to another community, the problem could resolve itself, or might be replaced by an even worse condition needing other procedures). In developing countries, expensive and advanced therapies are just not available. In other communities, the number of hospitals, MRI machines, and dialysis centers is limited, creating waiting lists and problems of availability.

4) Should one allocate care based on the patient's wealth? In this scenario, only patients who could afford the treatment could get it. This would be analogous to a two or three tiered system of care. Only those in the top tier could access restricted, expensive care. Although we believe every American is entitled to the best care in America, we recognize celebrities, government leaders, and the wealthy now receive faster and better care than the poor. We already have multi-tiered care, which we hate to admit.

5) Should there be a preset annual or lifetime monetary limit on the funds available for treatment? Such financial limits could be set for any procedure or individual. When that limit is reached, the patient or family must pay for additional expenses if they want continued treatment. Families might have to postpone medical attention until the following year's allotment was in place. Where such a system exists, each resident is issued medical vouchers or scripts annually. Vouchers are often sold (discounted) in the open market for needed cash or given to sicker family members. The original recipient is left medically vulnerable without available voucher payment for healthcare for him or herself. Should it be needed, new scripts would likely have to be purchased from whatever source. A

black market for health vouchers arose, and counterfeit vouchers appeared. A version of this policy would have the public deposit money in their own health account, which they would use when needed. There would be no funding when the account is exhausted or planned deposits are inadequate. The wealthy could afford longer and better care than those who could only save a fraction of what might be needed when ill.

6) Should we establish a lottery or sign-up sheet for expensive procedures? Delaying a procedure is a form of restricting availability. We now have waiting lists for organ transplantation based on organ availability, not finances. Or we can cap the number of expensive procedures permitted during a particular period.

7) Should we ration by the specific disorder? We could choose which conditions will be covered and which will not. We could let the insurance companies decide what they will or will not cover, then let the courts and judicial system arbitrate any disputes.

8) Should health insurance pay for the latest available medical advancements as they appear, such as stem cell transplants or gene transfer? As medical science develops new possibilities or cures, will these breakthrough treatments be available to all if the costs are excessive? But, in the end, how can anyone put a monetary value on human life or health? For the affected individuals and families, they are invaluable. Nonetheless, someone does make this determination; they must. That's their job.

As we now stand, insurance companies argue they will pay only for established and approved medical care. They will not pay for research, training, or any other care not directly involved with the care of their subscribers. Their policies determine the premiums they charge. This seems very reasonable. The conflict arises when a determination of experimental vs. established procedures is questioned. Even if new life-saving breakthrough therapies succeed, insurance carriers may claim these are experimental therapies that have yet to be widely used and established and, therefore, they will refuse to pay. These expensive new treatments were not in their calculus when their subscription premiums were set. Disputes must be decided by judicial or government intervention. As a consequence, our current healthcare system can delay the adoption of new treatments for years, at the cost of many lives. Consider having a newborn child with a rare genetic disorder that will cripple and shorten the child's lifespan, and knowing there appears to be a new, expensive "miracle" cure. Then having your health insurance company refuse to pay anything towards this treatment which they consider "experimental." These are all difficult situations to address humanely, and each society may develop different standards. However, one way or another, these issues must be addressed to ensure that a system of insurance exists that does not bankrupt the country's economy or curtail other needed services. These are societal issues, not purely medical ones.

Another kind of insurance that impacts the cost of healthcare is malpractice insurance. We are living in a litigious society where people look to profit from errors committed by mistake or incompetence. This pertains to institutions and all personnel involved in the patient's care. Purchasing malpractice insurance for all potential targetable individuals and general liability insurance significantly increases healthcare expenses. Unlike health insurance, which insures patients, malpractice insurance insures doctors and facilities from accusations of negligence. Usually, separate insurance companies sell this type of insurance. The cost of malpractice insurance depends on the financial limits chosen by the purchaser or demanded by the licensing authority and the anticipated risks based on prior settlement history. State authorities sometimes cover a portion of the insurance fees to help practitioners and institutions reduce their costs. Malpractice insurance is the most expensive for plastic surgery and orthopedics and the least for family medicine. As larger and larger settlements have been awarded, amounts for coverage and purchase costs have escalated. Having malpractice insurance with caps rising into the millions of dollars encourages more medical lawsuits. Costs for malpractice insurance spiraled upward, particularly for the surgical subspecialties and those performing medical procedures. Without a strong personal connection between doctor and patient, negligence lawsuits against doctors increased. To the patient, the provider was no longer their beloved doctor, and suing that person came with no hesitation or qualm. Lawyers charge nothing unless they win the case; therefore, the patient or claimant has little to lose by suing. Successful claims include payments for actual damages and expenses, pain and suffering, and punitive damages (usually much more than the actual damages). Negligence lawyers usually collect half of the award and are thus encouraged to inflate their demands. This is in keeping with the standard policy of having monetary awards as the goal, as well as the solace for the victim of improper care and the punishment for the individual responsible for such care. A more appropriate or logical approach would require the individual guilty of a negligent action to receive additional training and instruction to avoid repeating the error. The injured party certainly should have their actual expenses reimbursed and receive some penalty, but punitive damages must be contained. Lawyers might not endorse such a change.

The costs for international healthcare, both human and financial, have increased and have been made very public. The appearance of the Ebola virus and the rapid spread of COVID-19, HIV, Zika, and Influenza viruses in the U.S. illustrates how all humankind is at risk of contagious pathogens. People travel and spread microbes. Starvation, overcrowding, dehydration, and exposure to infections have global effects. Cleaning our water and food systems to prevent widespread medical problems is a national and international problem.

Crop failures, famine, loss of potable water, and climate change affect global healthcare. Air and water pollution obey no geopolitical boundaries. The spread of devastating infectious diseases threatens all living things. Governments and international agencies need increasing funds and must collect their revenues from their citizens. Nothing comes for free. A new medical or environmental problem elsewhere may lead to a medical crisis in the US. This crisis will put an unplanned strain on our economy and national budget. Uncertain costs are a concern for everyone involved in organizing medical care. We are all our brothers' keepers and must contribute to supporting national and international healthcare.

From prior experience, we have learned that when politicians recognize their constituents want changes in health insurance, they will likely act. The government still has the authority to oversee healthcare and exert pressure on private corporations. However, it needs to hear public demands and needs before it will respond. If dissatisfied with health insurance decisions, complacency can never produce change. Complaining to your representatives in government can.

Chapter 3
CHOOSING AND INTERACTING WITH YOUR MEDICAL TEAM

Your choice will not include those caring for you when hospitalized

Choosing your healthcare team can be stressful. Patients regularly discuss their doctors 'attributes with their friends at social gatherings, comparing the provider's skills, warmth, and how well the doctor deals with their concerns. Like trying a new restaurant, they may want to change their doctor if they have issues with the doctor's office or if they recently relocated and wish to find a doctor in a new community. It is an important decision for them, and they often spend a lot of effort researching candidates for this position. However, choosing a medical team is more than just choosing a doctor. The patient is choosing a medical network, a group consisting of a doctor, a medical assistant or nurse practitioner, and an office staff. Your choice will determine your covering doctors, specialist referrals, testing facilities, and even hospitals where your doctor may refer patients.

Frequently, your search begins with the doctor or the group that accepts your health insurance, illustrating the importance of funding and insurance before considering the doctor's attributes - money before competency. After acquiring several recommendations from trusted contacts, the next step is usually an internet search of potential providers, particularly for their educational credentials, patient reviews, insurance network affiliation, location, and personal data (such as age and gender). Your choice will depend upon which of these qualifications seems most important to you. Following this selection, the prospective patient makes a phone call to the doctor's office to inquire if the doctor still accepts their insurance, is taking on new patients, and how long the usual wait is for an appointment (initial and subsequent).

How are doctors rated? In most network practices, QR codes and multiple signs encourage patients to rate their doctor and the experience they had in the office. Doctors and staff see these signs prominently displayed throughout the office and feel these signs are a veiled warning intended to ensure patient satisfaction. However, their presence may be unsettling. It's like working in an office where the boss is noticeably watching you. While we do need some means to judge the performance of all healthcare system components, it is more difficult, nor is it encouraged, for patients to rate their insurance company or healthcare network. No codes or signs recommend rating satisfaction of these important entities. Doctors and office staff are targeted by this practice, which is a clear reminder to doctors of their loss of autonomy. Furthermore, this rating system by other patients is a poor way to judge the best doctor for you.

Everyone wants the "best doctor"! And who is the "best doctor"? Your internet search told you a lot about the provider's credentials and key interests, but does this enable you to decide? Should you choose the one with the most expensive office and location, believing the doctor must be good because of apparent wealth or success? Should you choose the doctor cited most in magazines as "one of the best" or the doctor of celebrities? Should you choose one based on the internet photo, the doctor's name, or educational background? In truth, there is no such thing as a "best doctor." Who is the best doctor for whom? Someone else's best doctor may not be the best for you. The best primary care doctor for you is one who makes you feel comfortable in your encounter and one in whom you have trust in their competence and judgment. You want a provider with a good knowledge of medicine, particularly regarding your concerns, an inquisitive mind who keeps learning, listens attentively to you, and can communicate even complex medical issues understandably and effectively. You want a doctor who you can understand, can explain medical information without using jargon, and is not dismissive of your requests. You want a doctor who respects you (the patient) as they would an equal, and you want a doctor who always has your best interests foremost in their recommendations. And you want a doctor who is not too embarrassed or afraid to say, "I don't know, but I will find out or request help if needed." This information is not obtained from an internet search, but this is your "best doctor." Remember that if you are dissatisfied with your choice, you can leave and find another doctor. When choosing a surgeon, you also are choosing an entire team that will care for you preoperatively, operatively, and postoperatively. A careless nurse or aide can cause many problems. You are choosing an institution and a network. After choosing a doctor, the question for you and the doctor is how often you should be seen and what regular testing should be done. Obviously, this depends on your general health and on your anxiety regarding your health. It also depends on your age and past medical history. A yearly examination is recommended for a healthy, young, or middle-aged individual. For the elderly and those with chronic medical diseases that need monitoring, more frequent visits are advisable. Regular medical visits serve the purpose of nurturing a more personal relationship between doctor and patient (where each understands the other) and are a way of discovering asymptomatic conditions that should not be ignored. Most health insurance plans now allow and finance an annual "wellness" visit, where there is no testing but a time where general concerns can be discussed.

Routine blood testing and early detection procedures are discussed in another section. For any test or procedure, the doctor must ask about the value of the testing vs. any potential harm. All tests and procedures have costs that will add to national healthcare expenditures. Electrocardiograms have no potential risk for harm and can disclose asymptomatic conditions. Annual EKGs are commonly done. Blood tests have more risk with venipuncture and have value, resulting in recommendations for annual testing of some routine blood values. X-rays have an accumulated risk of radiation toxicity and should be done more sparingly when a need is perceived. Some authorities recommend routine chest x-rays every 2-3 years. Other tests, like screening for blood in the stool or urine, are without risk, and annual screening is often recommended. Cancer screening and early detection of disease are discussed in another section.

Unfortunately, the best-made plans often go astray. We live in a world of managed care and unexpected happenings. Patients carefully investigate which physicians are on their insurance plan, only to discover the physician has since dropped out of that network (either party can sever their affiliation with any network at any time). Accidents also happen - anywhere and at any time. You are taken to a hospital where your doctors will be assigned to you: medical physicians and surgeons. All your research and interest in a particular medical team is nullified until you are discharged home. When hospitalized and in extreme need of medical care, your doctor will probably be an individual you never met, never chose, and one you know nothing about - a hospitalist employed by the hospital.

Despite all these potential obstacles to your plans, you still must choose the primary doctor for your care. Some individuals will make an appointment to screen a new doctor to see if they mesh, have a good rapport, and share a similar attitude regarding health and dying. Does the doctor seem rushed and eager to have you leave, as the doctor does have limited time to spend with a patient? This is of particular concern for older patients, who generally need more time with the doctor than younger patients. Older patients may need repetitive explanations until they understand what is being said. The elderly typically process information slower, have hearing issues, move more slowly, and have many more problems and worrisome issues to consider. Because older patients generally take far more physician time during an office visit and because the elderly may not have insurance coverage that reimburses or pays the doctor as well as wealthier, younger patients, many doctors try not to accept too many elderly patients into their practice (unless they are geriatricians).

A patient's advanced age does not increase insurance payments to doctors. Insurance does not pay by the number of organs or systems that need attention. But being older comes with all body parts and systems being older. Older patients have no young parts. After maturity, older parts usually do not function as well as previously. Natural aging produces changes that affect the heart, circulation, lungs, kidneys, and all organs. It's never a question of whether the patient has hardening of the arteries or decreased lung function. The question is, how significant are the natural changes of aging in affecting a person's life, and how much better would their life be if this problem could be mitigated? Discovery of an "abnormality" in an older person means little. Finding an abnormality in an older patient does not mean that it is the cause of their distress. It requires a judgmental decision about its impact on the patient's health. Furthermore, the patient's problem may be caused by many interacting difficulties, not any single abnormality. With their polypharmacy, older patients are at the greatest risk of medication-engendered contributions to their symptoms (see section on medications). Taking care of the elderly takes more time, more thought, and more involvement than caring for healthy younger patients. Geriatric medicine comes with many challenges, frustrations, and disturbing realities, but it can be gratifying to the practitioner who is not focused on becoming wealthy. Caring for the elderly forces the doctor to think about the patient as a whole and understand the clinical variables. It takes more time and effort but is intellectually more challenging. Being aware of these facts can reduce the patient's anger and resentment. Still, the patient should remember that your doctor is there for you, the patient; the patient is not there for the doctor. You are hiring the doctor to care for you and are really "the boss" (but don't push this point too hard).

Except in very rural communities, doctors participate in medical groups. They cover each other when one is on vacation or is not available. The doctor you choose may be your primary doctor, but your immediate illness may be referred to another in the group when your doctor is unavailable. The group hires receptionists and billing personnel and chooses which insurance they accept. Complaining to your primary doctor about any of these other services will require action by the group to effect changes affecting all members. Being in a group practice gives your doctor more clout and a louder voice in negotiations with insurance companies, medical organizations, and outside services, but at the cost of some personal autonomy.

Because insurance companies determine the fees of healthcare providers, many doctors will "drop out" of the insurance plan (even Medicare) if they feel their compensation is inadequate or the restrictions exerted by the insurance plan are too burdensome. Your insurance, be it private or Medicare, will not pay for any services performed by the doctor who has dropped out, nor will it pay for any laboratory costs for services ordered by that doctor.

The patient will then be responsible for the totality of the bill. It is, therefore, incumbent upon the patient to inquire about the insurance (including Medicare) accepted at the doctor's office before scheduling any visit. The receptionist making the appointment should, and usually will, tell the prospective patient if their insurance is accepted, but if they don't tell, you should ask. Still, some patients feel the visit to a particular doctor for advice, and their input is well worth the cost of an office visit, even without insurance reimbursement. More and more physicians are choosing to drop out of "regulated" medicine as more medicine is regulated by non-medical individuals with non-medical agendas. In dropping out of the health insurance system, doctors have returned to the simpler doctor-patient relationship that existed 50 years ago. These doctors are still licensed and must abide by governmental controls, but they are no longer managed by outside corporations telling them how they should practice medicine and how much they can charge the patient. They have reasserted control of how they want to conduct their own practice and care for patients. Many patients find this older doctor/patient relationship much more satisfying. The financial risk to the patient may seem prohibitive even when they realize that the major costs of hospitalization will still be covered by their health insurance. They will only have to pay the fees to that doctor and the cost of tests ordered by that doctor. As increasing numbers of doctors choose this path of reclaiming their professional independence, the costs to patients should become more affordable. No contract is signed, and patients can accept or reject this care as they choose.

Medical practitioners now include boutique or concierge doctors who sell slots in their practice for an annual fee that they set. These boutique doctors have chosen this option as another response to the limited insurance reimbursement for services fixed and set by health insurance companies. The fees for acceptance as a patient into the doctor's practice can be several thousands of dollars per patient annually to tens of thousands of dollars (an accepted medical expense for tax purposes). Patients must each enter and sign an annual contract with the boutique doctor, agreeing to the written terms. These doctors have stayed in the insurance system and will accept full insurance reimbursement without any residual fee or co-pay charges to their patients. This comes with a promise to limit their practice to a small, defined number of individuals, which should ensure more personal care. Any laboratory testing or procedures they order are covered by your health insurance, according to the terms of your policy. Boutique doctors provide their patients with their mobile cell numbers. The risk to the boutique doctor is acceptance of patients who may feel entitled to call the doctor at their whim (day or night) or be overly demanding. The doctor choosing to be "boutique" must also address what to do with the existing patients who choose not to be in the boutique pool. Should they have two sets of patients or drop those not wishing to be in the boutique group? The risk to the patient is that any other services not provided directly by their concierge doctor are not "concierge," or they are not receiving the personalized, attentive care they had expected. They must pay the copay for any laboratory or radiology tests ordered. The need for annual renewal gives each party a way out of their commitment.

Many Americans have chosen to select a cadre of specialists rather than a single primary care doctor for all their complaints. They see their specialists according to their symptoms, recognizing that the specialist will be more expert in their training and experience to manage their complaints than would any generalist. The difficulty is that the patient must diagnose any new complaint before selecting the specialist they think is best qualified to manage it. The downside of this plan is that specialists think first of disorders of their expertise and may not think of the patient as having other disorders or difficulties outside of their specialty. No one may be managing the patient as a whole and thinking outside the box. The patient should ask themselves which specialists they would call if they had a new medical issue. They need to identify which specialists they would want as their family's go-to doctor and ask that individual if they agree to take control of the patient's general care.

Having a primary care doctor (whether a family doctor, internist, or generalist) encourages a connection of mutual understanding. The interactions between the physician and patient are complex and unique. Although many features of the doctor/patient encounter depend on whether patients are visiting a primary care doctor, surgeon, psychiatrist, pediatrician, obstetrician, or therapist, some aspects of a medical visit are universal: it is a person seeking professional help and a healthcare provider doing their best to provide that help. Since doctors and patients are human, personalities and behavior influence their interactions. Physicians are trained to "do no harm." They try not to take chances and to be cautious in their treatment plans. As a result, they are more uniform in how they interact with their patients.

On the other hand, patients vary considerably in how they react to illness or pain; they may be hypochondriacal or cavalier in dealing with their symptoms. Patients can be fearful or reckless in their behavior. Some routinely exaggerate, while others minimize their complaints. Some reluctant patients are dragged unwillingly to see the doctor by a concerned family member, and they show their hostility. With repeated visits, the doctor learns what type of patient she or he is dealing with and how best to deal with that individual. It's advisable to bring a friend or relative with you to your medical appointment. A "second set of ears" helps mitigate the post-visit confusion the family may have. It also reduces the post-visit questioning of the patient with, "Did you mention you were having …such and such," or "What did the doctor say about …"? With the current EHRs, having patient portals where questions can be raised and answered, is helpful in this regard, but many elderly are uncomfortable with computers and portal interactions. Then, some patients prepare carefully for the visit, bringing a long list of symptoms they have accumulated since the previous visit, for which they want detailed explanations and discussion. You may see your doctor's eyes glaze over when you pull out the laundry list of complaints. It's best to confine your complaints to no more than 3 of the most important problems during a single visit, or nothing of value will be accomplished. Other complaints can have their turn during subsequent visits.

After several visits, the doctor learns to understand each patient and will individualize his or her approach. Some patients require much hand-holding and detailed explanations, and some quickly grasp what the doctor is saying and can integrate this information efficiently. Some patients panic with every medical disclosure, imagining the worst, and others feel they are immortal and will never get ill. Doctors have to know their patients. This is a learned process and will not happen when patients see different doctors with each complaint and medical visit. In the past, doctors practiced a form of paternalistic medicine where they, like a father figure, decided what information they would share with the patient. They decided whether the patient would benefit or be harmed by disclosure of the diagnosis or prognosis. The patient expects and will receive all pertinent information in today's world. It is their body, and they have the most right to know what is happening to and in their bodies.

Indicative of the times, a new patient's first question by the receptionist concerns their insurance, not their chief medical problem. But much more has changed in the past 50 years. The first encounter between the doctor and the patient traditionally followed a well-established routine. During the initial medical visit between the patient and the primary care doctor, the doctor must formulate a tentative diagnosis concerning the cause of the patient's complaints. Arriving at the proper diagnosis has always been vital. A thorough and thoughtful history achieves 70-80% of the tentative initial diagnosis. The physical examination garners another 15-20% of the diagnosis: inspection, palpation, and auscultation (listening with the stethoscope). The last 5-10% of the diagnosis is obtained with testing. Of these three components, obtaining the history takes the most physician time and acumen, physical examination of the patient consumes less time, and testing takes no physician time and little thinking. Payment for these services is inversely proportional to their importance and time consumption: testing costs the most and is the best remunerated, while physician time is the least financially rewarded. This encourages testing (see section below).

Nonverbal information flows continually during an encounter. Observation of the patient begins as soon as the physician sees the patient. The patient's appearance: is it appropriate, groomed, or neglected? Is the patient's bearing and manner confident, confused, or frightened? How easy was it for the patient to stand up from sitting, and was their gait and walk normal? Was there a normal arm swing while they walked? Did they require a cane or walker to move? How was their posture? Did they appear to be in pain or have shortness of breath while walking? Examining the soles of worn shoes could reveal an uneven pattern of wear that would disclose a gait problem, while wide stretching suggests swollen feet or edema. Looking at the worn notches of a belt can disclose whether the patient was losing or gaining weight. Loose or tight clothing may also disclose information about the patient's metabolic profile. Much information can be obtained by simple observation.

Talking to the patient also evaluates their hearing and the clarity of their speech and thinking. Was their speech slurred or crisp? Was there any asymmetry in their face, or did they favor one arm and hand over the other? How the patient interacted with their family or attendant provides clues to their social and psychiatric status and family dynamics.

All this information is obtained before even addressing the content of the interview, which questions the patient about their concerns, symptoms, and history. In listening to the patient relate their medical history, the physician must also judge how reliable and perspicacious a historian the patient is. How much do they understand about their own body? Does their history make sense? Is there something obvious they are avoiding or something they are hiding? This will provide clues to the reliability of their history and influence the doctor's later explanatory discussion with the patient (which must be conducted at a level the patient can absorb and comprehend).

As we learned medicine, we students practiced our observational skills while traveling on a subway or bus, making “subway diagnoses.” Obtaining a good medical history is vital to good patient care. As with an investigative reporter or detective, the doctor should assess the patient’s narrative and delve deeper into issues that need further clarification. The goal is not just to understand what the patient is saying but to understand the patient. What they are not saying can be equally or even more important than what they do say. The patient is asked what maneuvers alleviate or worsen the complaint. Had they had this complaint before? Is the symptom the problem, or is it the expression of an underlying problem? What else was happening in their life when the complaint began? By the end of the initial interview and history, the physician has already formulated an idea of the problem and what to explore during the next examination phase: the physical exam. The physician can spend more time and pay more attention to examining those systems more carefully, as the history suggests are abnormal.

Physical examination is structured and performed from the right side of the patient (the better side for examination of the abdomen for liver or spleen enlargement). The components of the physical examination are: Inspection (a close examination of the appearance of the affected area); Auscultation (listening with a stethoscope for sounds in the abdomen, chest, and circulation - blood flow through narrowed arteries creates different sounds called bruits); Palpation (feeling the affected area for lumps, masses, or tenderness; and Manipulation (testing movement and stiffness). A complete physical examination begins with examining the head and neck (including a fundoscopic examination of the eye and retina, along with an exam of the ear and auditory canal), chest, abdomen, and extremities. (The eye's retina is the only anatomical site where doctors can visualize the patient's arteries and veins without removing skin). Is there narrowing of the arteries, evidence of atherosclerosis, hemorrhages, or signs of increased blood pressure? Much can be learned by examining the fundus [back] of the eye). Palpating and listening to blood flow in the carotid arteries can suggest vascular and cardiac problems. Observation of the jugular veins in the neck for distention and pulsations also tells us about potential heart abnormalities. The physical examination includes testing neurological function, muscular, motor, and sensory functions, special senses, and skin eruptions. A complete exam evaluates joint rigidity, flexibility, and signs of inflammation (heat, redness, tenderness, and swelling). A neurological exam, testing for sensory or motor nerve dysfunction, is important, as is a mental status exam in select patients. Rectal and pelvic examinations for prostatic or gynecological disorders are included for completeness.

Only after a good history and physical examination can the physician selectively choose which tests are needed to confirm or refute the doctor's tentative diagnosis: the differential diagnoses. That is the purpose of testing (again, refer to the section below). After arriving at a tentative diagnosis, the physician decides on a treatment plan. Are they treating the complaint, the disorder, the patient, or all three?

Now, we come to how today's doctor-patient interaction is often performed. Covid-19 came with its demands for isolation and avoidance of physical contact. Insurance companies encouraged and paid for medical examinations through "Zoom" or computers. Zoom meetings have an attractive side. There is no need to dress formally or travel. A person can have a cup of coffee or a snack during the encounter. The exam is done in the comfort of a patient's (and sometimes doctor's) home, and the risk of preventing the spread of an infectious disease is avoided.

However, with Zoom, we bypass the observation and historical aspects of the examination. A doctor cannot observe the patient walking or any of the above mentioned characteristics; a physical exam is impossible. Only minimal information can be obtained, focused only on the immediate complaint. During office visits, time is critical, and the Zoom visit is abbreviated and usually focuses on the main complaint(s) only.

Additional concerns involve fundamental aspects of human nature. Patients almost always have some element of stress, anxiety, and fear when seeing their doctor. Will something horrible be revealed? Will this visit result in painful procedures, hospitalization, or the discovery of a fatal or crippling disorder? Patients may wince when they see their doctor wearing an examination glove, fearing what the doctor plans to do. How much money will be charged for this examination and its aftermath? How much of the bill will the insurance pay? Will my illness cause me to lose or be unable to continue my employment? How will my family cope with the results of this exam? "I feel well. Why does the doctor have to go into all these other issues?" Of course, if, in a cursory examination, the doctor missed something important, the patient will likely sue the doctor. A good doctor is looking out for the patient's well-being and health, not just responding to the patient's complaint. The patient is not expected to be the doctor. Such evaluations may disclose serious disorders in an early stage, to the patient's surprise and benefit. The doctor may also worry about missing something that proves to be essential and will be practicing defensive medicine. Questions of this sort race through the doctor's mind. Although these questions may arise during a human-to-human interaction, they will most likely not be addressed during a Zoom meeting.

Most doctors have had the experience of a patient initially complaining of something trivial. Then, as they are about to leave (after a half-hour or hour encounter), they mention casually having had chest pain, passing out, or coughing blood. This comes out almost as an afterthought but was probably the primary purpose of the visit. They may initially have hesitated to mention this important detail for many psychological reasons and fear. They developed the confidence to address this critical issue only at the end of the visit. It was a "now or never" moment. At this time, the doctor knows the next patient in the waiting area is already becoming impatient and recognizes they are running late. But how can the doctor postpone the evaluation of these significant complaints? Can the doctor even suggest the patient return another day when something serious may be happening? Or how, after an extended visit, can the doctor recommend the patient go to a hospital Emergency Department before evaluating the complaint?

As mentioned above, it is very helpful for patients to bring a companion on their visits, mainly if they are elderly. Having an extra set of ears is very helpful, as patients often "tune out" after the first suspicions the doctor enunciates. The companion's role is to remain composed and be an objective observer. Doctors now usually provide the patient with a written summary of the visit for this purpose and copies of their test results. EHRs are now required to contain a patient portal. This allows the patient to see their test results and make appointments. Some patients, though, do not do well with computer portals. Zoom encounters are less likely to address these latter issues, and, as discussed above, computer programs may be challenging for the elderly to use.

Office visits are now scheduled by non-medical personnel. Making an appointment by phone with your doctor can be a prolonged, frustrating experience; getting a professional answer to a question may be an all-day ordeal. Reaching the proper person capable of understanding the problem and providing an appropriate response can take hours of waiting for a call-back or an available operator. Again, computer portal interactions can be faster but may require advanced computer skills. A simple phone call to your doctor is rarely an option. You seldom get through to the doctor. In private offices, doctors tell the scheduler how much time they expect the visit to require. The doctor controls the time spent with any patient. In group practices, the group establishes a standard schedule. Often, it's 30-60 minutes for a new patient and 15-20 minutes for a follow-up or established patient. The office practice fixes these time constraints, and group practice doctors must abide by the limitations. Running overtime is frowned upon, as another doctor may be waiting for the examination room; if the visit is not concluded in time, the patient must schedule a return visit to finish the current visit. The difficulty is that doctors never know beforehand how long the visit will need to address the patient's complaint(s), even when the visit is supposedly routine.

With difficulty making the appointment, getting to the medical office, and waiting for the doctor to see them, it's understandable why patients frequently feel irritated when they feel rushed through a superficial encounter with the doctor. Consequently, some patients then bring up more issues they wish to discuss thinking that since they had to wait, let the next patient wait, or this is how I can punish the doctor for the time I sat in the waiting room. "Even if not necessary, I want my full 15-20 minutes."

Much of the changes in the doctor-patient relationship are a result of specialization. Primary care doctors (in internal medicine or pediatrics) are the gatekeepers of medical care. They are usually the first line of care to evaluate patients with medical concerns. They may feel comfortable managing the case alone or refer the patient to a specialist if they feel inadequate or need confirmation. We expect the primary care doctor to be knowledgeable about a broad base of medical information to make the appropriate initial decisions. Specialists are expected to have a much narrower focus of interest and be experts in their particular specialty. Their knowledge base is usually restricted in scope but deep in their field.

In contrast to how medicine was practiced decades ago, both types of medical care are needed to meet the medical needs of patients today. In theory, the specialist is a consultant to the primary care doctor and reports his or her feelings to the referring doctor, who then makes the final decisions (with the patient's approval): agreeing with or rejecting the specialist's recommendations. This policy is now rarely followed. Rejecting a specialist's recommendations may look ill-advised in a malpractice lawsuit. Patients often have several specialists they use for their particular concerns, and they choose which one to see according to their chief concern at the time.

Oddly, despite many patients visiting specialists, others are moving in the opposite direction. Their care is mainly in the hands of nurse practitioners and medical assistants. Like medics in the military or feldschers in developing countries, these practitioners are trained to manage common medical concerns, are paid less, and fill the gap created by a shortage of trained physicians. Most medical problems are uncomplicated, and the patient doesn't need a professor to manage them. The value of the assistant is appreciated by patients and physicians alike. However, adding more practitioners and personnel to an office staff results in even less personal contact time between the patient and physician.

Despite the changes in medical care, the patient's medical needs have remained the same. When they enter the world of the hospital, they may feel they have entered a foreign land where they don't understand the language, the environment, or the actions of people around them. They have lost control of their life and are often infantilized to the degree that they depend upon others for almost all their basic needs. They may feel they are being treated as objects, not humans. They are a small cog in the enormous universe of medical care. And this occurs when they are uncertain about their finances, social status, and life. Each day, they may fear what the next day will bring.

In the helpless and uncertain state of the hospitalized patient, patients must have absolute trust in the competence, motivation, and commitment to their welfare by everyone caring for them, even when this involves total strangers. Being confined to a bed, it's hard for a patient to be their own advocate. They must rely on the assistance of unfamiliar staff to be their surrogates. In the past, it was the family doctor who assumed this responsibility. For the medically unsophisticated patient, it can be terrifying. And for those not speaking English, even more so. In the past, the visits by their family doctor brought a great sense of relief and assurance. This was someone they knew and trusted: someone who sat down and explained what was happening in a way they could understand. Although they may not recognize it, most ill or dying patients seek their mothers' loving warmth and comfort. Now, with hospitalists, nurses, and other hospital staff, who they never chose and who know little about them as a person, caring for them, they need to trust total strangers. Having their doctor pull up a chair and sit beside their bed is reassuring to the patient. It means the doctor is interested in talking to them and is not planning to rush away to another patient or a golf course after the initial greeting.

Today, having their family doctor visit them in the hospital is a luxury. It is a social visit only. The family doctor cannot write orders or override what the hospitalist is planning. Insurance will not pay for two doctors seeing the patient on the same day. The family doctor will not be paid and will not submit a bill for the time and effort of visiting the hospitalized patient. The hospitalist is the assigned doctor of record - the managing attending. To the hospital and the insurance company, the hospitalist, not the family doctor, is the doctor of record, caring for the patient. Thus far, the hospital and the staff have tried their best to assuage patient fears and instill trust between themselves and the patient. With the further corporatization of healthcare, will this erode faster?

Patients today occasionally interact with their doctors in the office as if they felt the doctor was their employee (which the doctor is, but should not be felt to be such) or an extension of the insurance plan or medical facility they dislike. Patients can be rude, demanding, abusive, and inconsiderate. They may manifest displeasure at how the insurance company handles their coverage or are annoyed at how much effort it has been to reach their doctor by phone. They may be annoyed by their long wait before being seen but do not want to feel rushed when they finally meet their doctor. Never mind the next patient upset by how long the doctor spends with them and listening to their venting. They are dissatisfied and frustrated by how their medical care is being conducted. These may all be reasonable reactions, but patients should not take this out on their doctor. The doctor is probably also frustrated and is the patient's ally, not their adversary. Doctors may already feel the system is using them, and when patients act up, it makes things worse; they feel abused. With all the years of education and expense involved in becoming a physician, all the years of practicing medicine, being treated as an expendable employee and not a professional is most demeaning. Most doctors entered the healthcare professions as a calling, a desire to be of service and help their fellow humans as best they can.

Doctors have lost much of their autonomy, and most feel controlled and over regulated by corporate decisions. They may sense their profession is becoming less of a profession and more of a trade. They often feel disrespected by the system. Showing some empathy and concern for your doctor improves your relationship. However, doctors are trained to deal with difficult, angry, and frustrated patients in the same professional and caring way they would with pleasant and friendly ones. It is hoped that doctors choose the profession of medicine for the satisfaction of helping patients, irrespective of income and any adulation. Doctors have managed patients with paranoia and other psychiatric problems, dementia, disabilities, and handicaps of all varieties. In the Oath of Maimonides, doctors swear, "May I never see in the patient anything but a fellow creature in need." Physicians are not supposed to judge but to treat all patients equally. Patients should never feel guilty about being unwell. They never asked to be sick. And doctors should never become angry or impatient with sick or distraught patients because of their disease. However, patients who act up by choice or try to take advantage of the doctor are a different case.

I suspect all doctors have tried to evaluate and examine disturbed patients who try to bite and scratch them and resist examination. I certainly have. Distressed patients and children may try to prevent their blood pressure from being measured or stop the doctor or lab assistant from trying to draw blood or insert an IV. The family or attendant accompanying the patient may try to restrain the patient and apologize for the patient's unruly behavior. I remind them that it's not the patient but the disease that's acting badly. We should not take it out on the patient. We don't get angry or physically attack a child in a temper tantrum or a wild adult. We learn to do our best with patients who can't communicate due to language or speech issues. Treating patients with dementia, speech difficulties, and physical handicaps requires much more time and effort than caring for healthier, younger patients. The wild behavior may be a consequence of the underlying disorder or because the patient is terrified and needs some calming reassurance. Time allotments and payments, however, do not reflect these situations. The doctor will run late and behind schedule when patients need more time. But that's what medical care is.

Patients visit doctors for various reasons: they feel sick, they need advice about their health status, they need regular monitoring of their treatment, and they visit for social reasons. For many isolated and lonely elderly people, the visit to their doctor is an important social event where they will interact with an adult who listens to them and takes their complaints seriously. The visit has an important salutary effect.

Doctors in private practice have no obligation to accept every patient. Patients also have the right to find another doctor at their own discretion. Physicians have the credo of never abandoning a patient in need. They can transfer care to another health provider when possible and try to assist a patient in finding another physician when they can no longer care for the patient. This policy holds true even under Good Samaritan conditions, where the physician will stay and provide care in an emergency until relieved by an EMT or other medical personnel. It may be more challenging and difficult to care for some patients, but doctors take an oath to do their best to help all their patients, regardless of who they are or how they are behaving. That forms the basis of the doctor's creed.

Doctors tarnish their public image (and the profession's image) when they appear more interested in personal profit than the patient's welfare. Hospital visits, for which insurance is billed, should be more than a wave to the patient from the door. Even though the doctor may have discussed the patient's case with other doctors, consultants, and nursing staff and reviewed the notes, test results, and current EHR entries, this was not a satisfactory visit from the patient's perspective. They anticipate the doctor is there to visit them personally, not their chart or EHR. The patient may have been waiting anxiously for the doctor's daily visit when they will learn about their status and understand what has been transpiring. The doctor's role should be to explain to the patient what has been happening and what to expect in the future. The doctor should inquire about any new difficulties the patient is experiencing and provide a personal touch and assurance. As the principal professional link with what is happening to the patient in the hospital, the doctor's role is to keep the patient informed about all matters that affect their condition. The doctor should be trying to assuage the patient's fears. When physicians spend more time caring for the medical record than they do with the patient, they dehumanize the patient.

A relatively new aspect of medical service has surfaced at the interface of medicine with social, legal, and ethical issues. Physicians are trained to deal with health and disease and do their best for their patients. Now, doctors are asked to be involved with death, as in physician-assisted suicide, participating in executions of death penalty inmates, and with the consequences of legal abortions. Physicians have no special education, training, or qualifications to judge or participate in the complex roles they are asked to perform. As humans, they each have their own moral compass and sense of social responsibility. Social and legal issues should be left to the lawyers, judges, clergy, and politicians. Savvy doctors avoid making decisions that administrators, lawyers, or judges best handle. Health personnel should stick to medical details. That's where their expertise lies.

Chapter 4
VALUE AND SIGNIFICANCE OF TESTING

What happens when the tests look better, but the patient is worse?

Were we treating the test results or the patient?

Laboratory testing is the most impersonal component of healthcare; it's based on machines evaluating some small specimen of material removed from the patient. If we add testing procedures, such as ultrasounds and x-rays, they become the most lucrative aspect of healthcare. Placing a value or cost for a laboratory test or procedure is a simple, uncomplicated task for computers and insurance companies. The testing consists of fixed, repetitive, verifiable constants with machines performing defined activities or usually a technician trained to use a specific machine. Such tests and procedures are the same anywhere they are performed in the country or in the world. No human cognitive activity or variables complicate the components: they are the most impersonal aspects of healthcare. Interpretation of results is another matter. Insurance carriers and algorithms love tests.

Testing had never been the central focus of medical care; it was mostly a supplement to confirm or refute a tentative diagnosis. Today, testing seems to have become paramount; patients expect testing and request it be done. Testing emerged as a significant component of care as patients requested and anticipated more and more testing, and testing proved to be very remunerative. Patients learned to focus on the importance and value of test results from their doctors: taking cues from their care providers. "If the doctors are doing all these tests, the tests must be very important." And why do doctors now order so many tests? The incentive to order laboratory tests began during the doctor's medical schooling and early training. Being unsure and lacking confidence in their medical acumen, junior doctors were afraid of being humiliated during morning attending doctor rounds with their professors and fellow students. What if the attending doctor asked the young doctor, "How is the patient's liver or kidney function today?" and the student or house staff doctor didn't know? You could never be sure what questions you would be asked. It is better to know a lot of laboratory results that you could spout that would impress your colleagues and teaching attending during morning teaching rounds.

In evaluating how a hospitalized patient is responding to treatment, assessing their bodily functions is equally, if not more important than any laboratory test result. This is rarely stressed and underappreciated. There are no code numbers or fees associated with these observations. Are they sleeping, toileting (urine and bowels), eating, and moving? Are they in pain, and how is their affect? Are they losing weight? Are they able to get out of bed or need help with their basic body functions? These are all important aspects of a hospitalized patient's well-being, and cost the system nothing. They are of greater clinical importance than a blood test number. If there is a change in a patient's general status, the doctor must judge whether it is an effect of a medication or a change in their disease. Nurses are in the best position to assess the daily status of any patient in their care. Nurses see the hospitalized patient several times a day and are well aware of subtle changes in the patient's behavior and condition. The food delivery attendant knows if the patient is eating or finishing their meal and how much fluid they drink. An attendant emptying a bedpan or urinal is well acquainted with the patient's toileting. The nurse caring for the patient should know these answers and more. They are the best source of information about daily alterations in the patient's general condition; a more objective observation than that offered by the patient, whose subjective feelings may be unreliable.

Questioning the nurse provides much information about the patient's status and educates the nurse about what the doctor thinks is important and what they should assess. Hospital nurses may be busy, but can also be a good source of information to the family if they are available.

Patients are impressed and even obsessed with test results and procedures. This is not to say that testing is not a valuable tool in medical care. Test results are valuable markers for investigating a disease's progress and clues to therapy's potential adverse effects. However, today's fascination with test results displayed by many patients is alarming and is something recent. Must the same test be repeated daily or twice daily? Sometimes the answer is, "Yes." But often it is done routinely and not needed at that frequency. Before ordering any tests, doctors must weigh how the results will alter their recommendations. Not every abnormality needs to be addressed. There is the "So What" principle. If an abnormality is discovered, "So What?" What should be done? The need for attention and treatment of any abnormality depends on how it will improve the patient's life or what it signifies, balanced against any suspected risk. And it is the patient who can best assess the benefits and risks to themselves, not the provider. They must know why the test is needed and give consent for the test. The patient must understand their options to make this assessment. It is the job of the doctor to make sure the patient understands the facts before consenting (making an informed consent). For example, would the discovery of osteoporosis by a bone density evaluation alter the management of a patient dying with advanced kidney failure, cancer, or dementia? And if a patient inquired about their lead or copper levels, would the doctor not question why the results of these tests are needed? Doctors frequently order testing to protect themselves against malpractice lawsuits and comply with patient wishes. It's a sad commentary, but doctors must also practice defensive medicine in today's litigious world. Anticipating a possible lawsuit, doctors consider how any action or nonaction on their part could be used against them in a court of law. Appropriate documentation and laboratory or radiological evaluations are critical in legal defense. In litigations accusing doctors of negligence, blame is often directed at failing to recognize a dangerous medical condition through inadequate testing. You never hear of doctors being accused of ordering too much testing.

Patients frequently request copies of their test results, which often engenders increased anxiety. In the past, when X-ray films were used, doctors gave patients their old X-rays. Patients often asked me what they should do with the old films they stored in their closets. Their true value is for comparative examination when looking at future films (there was also silver that could be extracted from the films). In today's world, X-rays are not on film but reside on computers or disks. Patients are now given CDs that contain their films. I often wondered what patients did with all their accumulated outdated laboratory results. If visiting a new doctor, only the last several results are relevant, and outdated results can usually be obtained by contacting the laboratory directly. Doctors don't need volumes of old laboratory results. They don't fit into the patient's EHR in any case.

Test results are frequently accompanied by a computer-generated interpretation of statistically low (L) or high (H) results outside the average range (one standard deviation from the mean, which will encompass 95% of results). I frequently explained that if 100 tests are taken on a perfectly normal person, five results will likely be outside one standard deviation and get an L or H designation. One test result of the 100 will be two standard deviations from the mean (1%). That's just simple statistics and expected in a perfectly normal distribution of results. The word "abnormal" literally means outside the normal range. It does not mean there is a problem requiring immediate attention. The next point is to explain that a single test result is not usually what patients want or what the doctor focuses on. We all want to know the **significance** of the finding, not just the number. This is not usually obtained from a single test result. It's the change in value over time that has the most meaning. If an X-ray or blood test discloses an abnormality, what does that represent? Although patients often ask, "What does that result mean?", they really want to know what it signifies; are they sick or in trouble? For that answer, it's best to have comparative data. The questionably abnormal test result must be seen in perspective and compared to previous results (if any are available). If there has been no change in the "abnormality" in 6 months, one year, or five years, it can't be very significant if the patient has no accompanying symptoms and the patient can be reassured. If the "abnormal" value is normalizing, there is less need for concern, but it does provide evidence of something getting better.

Further evaluation is needed if the "abnormal" value is new or worsening, especially if it correlates with the patient's symptoms or disease. If no previous results are available for comparison, the doctor will likely request another test in 2-3 weeks for future comparison. Having comparative values analyzed over time allows for better extrapolation and understanding of the progression or resolution of the condition. There is also some normal variability in results. If the same test were repeated on a daily basis, small variability in values will be obvious (some slightly higher and some slightly lower). Alterations in a person's state of hydration and inherent alterations in testing are the usual cause, and of no concern.

There has to be a purpose to testing, more than just ordering tests indiscriminately to find an abnormality that can be further evaluated. This is like throwing stuff against the wall to see what sticks. Doctors must be selective in ordering medical tests and procedures. Tests are expensive; therefore, ordering unnecessary tests is wasteful and increases the national cost of healthcare considerably. Being tested is also not fun for the patient. Even in routine screening, we don't want to order "everything."

What is driving the need for all this testing? Is it the monetary reward realized by testing, or were the tests requested for legitimate medical concerns? Had the doctors been "pushed" or encouraged to order more tests for financial benefit (relative value units, or RVUs), medical and legal defense issues, or were they following the patients' or their administrators' requests? Patients have asked, "If blood is being taken, why not test for everything? It's free, and I have good insurance. It won't require another needle stick." They would have already experienced the pain of venipuncture. "What's the problem with removing another tube of blood?"

"What's the problem?" First, testing is expensive. Even when insurance pays for the testing, none of this is "free!" Someone is paying for the tests, and the costs will eventually filter down to the consumer or taxpayer. Secondly, there is no "everything." The benefit has to justify the price, whether it be blood, x-rays, scans, or procedures such as stress tests or endoscopies. Indiscriminate testing has little benefit but increases the cost of health care. But more importantly, with greater and more sensitive testing, small irregularities will always be found. It's like looking at your car's finish with a magnifying glass. Small scratches, dings, and blemishes will be seen. Small blemishes don't affect the car's performance, and it is unnecessary to attend to them. The same holds true in medicine. We don't have to treat every skin blemish;

abnormal tests may be considered internal blemishes. It's the "So What" principle again. With advanced MRI screening, small scars or irregularities are frequently detected and called "incidental" findings. The closer and more carefully you look, the more differences you will find. A portion of these will be tagged as abnormal (meaning unusual). Batteries of blood tests may disclose results outside the normal expected distribution. "So what?" With aging, more and more "abnormalities" will be found. This leads to the question of what to do with these incidental "abnormal" findings: ignore them, follow them with repeated testing, or refer them to specialists for more advanced evaluation or surgical intervention? The patient may see multiple specialists within a very short time and may be referred for more advanced testing. It can quickly become a snowball effect that consumes and takes over the patient's life. Fearing the worst, it can destroy the patient's and the family's life pleasures, eating away at their sleep and composure. They are sacrificing valuable time looking into something that may not be real, or untreatable.

These "abnormal" findings may just reflect the patient's unique self. They may be features of the patient's genetic heritage. They may be the scars of previous events that went unrecognized, or they even have been born with these "abnormalities". Still, the consequences of the unexpected findings can have a devastating financial and life-consuming effect that frightens the patient and the family unduly. Will the abnormality, now considered trivial by their doctor, grow into something major? While the doctor may believe the incidental findings are insignificant, no one can be absolutely certain. Doctors do make errors in their opinions and decisions. They are human. The patients will see these abnormal results and worry.

To make matters worse, for completeness, reports from radiologists and pathologists may include references to possible frightening disorders their studies suggest. They are protecting themselves from litigation by raising the remote possibility that there may be tumors or other serious conditions they missed. These reports appear on patient portals and frighten the patient unnecessarily. Patients may want and demand further investigation and request that everything be done to ensure no serious condition exists. Should they see more specialists? “If my doctor is not taking these abnormalities seriously, should I find another doctor?” When nothing in the history or physical examination suggests any active problem, a test casually added to the orders has become a major medical calamity. An “abnormal” test result doesn’t come with an explanation of why it is abnormal. The doctor is trapped, and the patient may be distressed over nothing significant. The final medical cost for evaluation can be astronomical (financially and personally) just because the patient wanted “everything tested.” In a very short time, patients get nuclear scans, MRI and MRA scans, and ultrasounds. They are seeing specialists of all disciplines. New studies may find further questionable abnormalities that trigger further testing.

In discussing how to evaluate results labeled abnormal with patients, it’s best to consult them about how far they wish to go. “What if exploratory surgery or invasive procedures were required to biopsy the suspicious area?” Procedures could be uncomfortable and costly to them, even when their insurance paid most of the bill. Any surgical procedure brings its own accompanying risk of adverse consequences, which patients must acknowledge in their consent. Patients usually prefer to wait and follow the abnormality with another test in a reasonably short interval. It’s the old can of worms or sleeping dog story. It becomes a matter of accepting some risk. We cannot avoid taking risks in life or in medical care.

We take risks daily when a person stands up, walks, or gets into a car. We know that bad things can happen without warning at any time. In medicine, we can't prevent bad things from happening; they will. But we try to be prepared and respond to medical surprises appropriately when they occur. The sad truth is that aging and death are inevitable, and a morbid fear of dying can lead to a fear of living: a fear of going to unfamiliar places or trying new things.

People who fear taking risks miss out on many of life's pleasures. However, a reasonable amount of caution in life and medicine is appropriate. The doctor and patient should discuss a plan to respond to the unlikely possibility of the small molehill becoming a mountain. The discussion will reassure the patient that the doctor is not dismissing the abnormal finding out of hand. Significant problems will soon declare themselves. Screening for latent conditions is valuable but needs justification and reason for need, not just for passing interest. It sounds simple. Patients should not fear **suggesting** a test, but all testing should be rational, practical, and justifiable.

Reimbursement for tests and procedures is much greater than that paid for the doctor's time and thinking. Patients only have to look at the insurance payment receipts they receive in the mail (EOBs or explanation of benefits). The charges and payment for the average office visit may be $150.00, but the laboratory tests done that day might be charged ten times as much ($1500.00). It is easy to confirm a test was done if there was any question of fraud. The charge for the test is fixed and routine, making it simple for reimbursement purposes. It is far more difficult to validate the time and effort placed on the doctor-patient interaction or place a monetary value on cognitive effort. Insurance companies rarely, if ever, question payment for testing.

In medical offices and clinics, new testing machines were always desirable. That's what brings in the revenue. And when an expensive machine is purchased, it has to be used. Doctors in that practice are encouraged to order those tests and procedures that utilize those machines. This also impresses the patients. Patients often told me how modern and good some other medical offices were; they had all these new machines that they used regularly. The office was well-equipped and up-to-date. Patients accepted and relished all the testing. People are impressed with advanced machines and their technological capabilities. People are seduced by technology. But machines are machines; they don't think for themselves. They are tools to be used wisely by those who understand their function, faults, limitations, and values. There are always false positive and false negative test results that must be considered. Testing facilities and machines are not for patients to admire and want testing or treatment. They are important tools to be used when the indication requires. On the other hand, the money involved in testing and the keen interest and wonder of the public in advanced testing stimulates research and development of the next generation of testing.

It's natural for people to be fascinated with test results. Here is something concrete in the medical field that they can truly comprehend. It's not something they need a medical degree to understand. It's usually written in numbers, not professional jargon. They can engage with the doctor about a finding that both are dealing with at a similar level. And they can easily follow the progression or improvement in any abnormal laboratory value.

Medical facilities need revenue, and follow the rule of going where the money flows. A colonoscopy that takes 45 minutes to accomplish may be reimbursed at a rate far less than the pathological examination of the polyp that took one minute to remove and a minute to analyze. An echocardiogram performed by a technician can bring in more revenue than a long visit with a cardiologist. Interpreting an X-ray by a radiologist can take less than a minute but is handsomely compensated. Testing and doing procedures are the most lucrative aspects of medicine. Even in large medical centers, the Departments of Radiology, Clinical Pathology (or Laboratory testing), and Surgery, with its attendant pathological examination of surgically removed tissue, are the revenue engines. The medical doctor, caring for the patient, is merely the vehicle for ordering the tests. The primary care doctor is the vehicle for referral to the specialist who brings in the greatest revenue.

The cart is now pushing the horse. The focus on testing and procedures has changed how medicine is practiced. And patients and insurance providers have bought into this arrangement and endorsed it. Doctors in private practice who do minimal testing and few or no procedures can't survive financially in today's world if they accept insurance payments. Their overhead can equal or exceed their income in solo private practice, where they must pay for their malpractice insurance, rent, and staff. They must be supported in larger institutions where they will make the referrals and order the tests and procedures that keep the business afloat. New machines and newer procedures bring in larger profits.

This policy favors advanced specialty training over general medicine for medical students. The specialist who performs procedures will earn a far greater income than the general practitioner, internist, geriatrician, pediatrician, or psychiatrist whose practice does not include procedures. With the likelihood of having a large debt from student loans for many years of education and training, there is a financial incentive to perform tests and procedures as often as can be justified, even if the results are not essential or needed at that frequency.

Chapter 5
UNDERSTANDING MEDICATIONS

What's in a name, a prescribed schedule, and warning labels? Information overload is dangerous when it confuses and frightens the patient

Taking medications appropriately is a major source of confusion and difficulty for many patients, particularly the elderly with arthritis in their hands, poor vision, tremors, a need to take multiple medications at different schedules, and differing appearance of generic medications. Older individuals take at least three different prescription drugs and some "over-the-counter" medicines. If donating blood, they must alert the phlebotomist of the medicines they are taking, as these will be transfused into the recipient of their blood.

As people age, their metabolism slows, and they eliminate medicines (and even body proteins) more slowly. Consequently, the medicines circulate in their active state for a longer period of time. This can result in a slow increase in the functional levels of the drug or hormone. If a person does not eliminate the previous day's drugs completely before taking the next day's aliquot, circulating drug levels will rise. This is particularly important when hormones or some medications are taken for years without checking their levels. Your body may be struggling to compensate for what effects the accumulated drugs are having, or you will feel the consequences.

As a rule, older patients taking drugs for years need a reduction in dosage and/or an increase in the interval between administrations (half the dose at twice the interval). Similarly, the condition for which the medicines were initially prescribed may no longer be a problem, but somehow, no one told them to stop. Their body has adapted to this drug. Periodic reevaluation of the need for medications should be undertaken rather than just continuing the drug regimen automatically because the patient is tolerating them.

Some simple and avoidable mistakes in taking medicines are commonly made, and most can be avoided. Labels can be confusing, particularly if generic medications are substituted for brand names. If this happens, a simple colored label or tag can be placed on the bottle, identifying its purpose and giving instructions on when and how to take it properly. If taking two different strengths of the same medicine (as in the case of thyroid hormone when a single tablet may not be of the desired strength), keep the medications in separate bottles with different tags. Although it may be easier to carry on your person, try not to put different medications into the same bottle or pill bag when traveling (the problem of loose unlabeled pills leads to many errors). If you forget or miss taking a particular medicine one day, don't panic or "double up" the next day to compensate for the day missed. Understand if any medicines you take are diet-dependent or stress-dependent (such as diabetes medicines or antihypertensives) **significant** alterations in your diet or activity will affect your medication requirement on the days affected. The dosage of these medicines is based on their immediate need, and since your blood sugar and blood pressure change with the amount of sugar or salt in your diet, you may need adjustments in your prescriptions when you change your diet. However, since your diet changes daily, your prescriptions must reflect an average or general trend in controlling your blood pressure or diabetic status. An important detail to recognize is that your diet and stress as a patient in a hospital are much different from that at home. The amount of cortisol and adrenaline you produce will vary. This may account for a change in your routine medications in the hospital, where your immediate need determines your medications. Don't run out of medication and wait till the next doctor's appointment before asking for refills. And, if your doctor had given you free samples or a small amount of a medicine to "try its effect," make sure you are still taking that medicine when you next see your doctor. If that medicine is out of your system during your next examination, its benefit or harm will be impossible to determine.

Medicines are expensive (even with co-pays), and saving on medication costs can be a priority. Pharmaceuticals are most expensive in the US, and many people search the internet for cheaper medicines from abroad. Drug manufacturers rightly argue that the cost of research and development (R and D) of new medicines is enormous and that only a small fraction of developed drugs ever reach the market. Most new drugs are discarded during their development and are a total financial loss. Pharmaceutical firms claim that this justifies the high price of those that reach the pharmacy. This is partly true, and the FDA gives pharmaceutical firms a 6-year exclusivity period for their brand name drug, during which no competitive generics can be licensed. Still, some challenge this argument. Some medications are developed abroad and brought here after showing efficacy and safety. US manufacturers did not waste a fortune on their R and D. Other new drugs are "me-toos." Another manufacturer spent a small fortune developing a new class of drugs and marketed this "groundbreaking" medication. Competitive manufacturers recognize the need and potential market for this new medication, already know its problem side effects, composition, and chemical formula, and invest in modifying it to create a new product (sometimes better than the original one). They did not bear the same cost for its development as the original product required. But they, too, charge a considerable amount for their drug. Such was the case with statins, widely used to control cholesterol levels. After Mevacor (Lovastatin) was released, other pharmaceutical firms rushed to produce Simvastatin, Atorvastatin, Pravastatin, Rosuvastatin, and Pitavastatin. A third argument concerning the high cost is that older generic drugs can also be expensive. Pharmaceutical manufacturers complain that reducing their prices by governmental pressure or law would discourage the development of future medications. This, too, is true, but how much profit can they justify with this argument? The most likely explanation for the high cost of US drugs is the profit motive - greed. This is supported by the jump in the cost of Adrenalin (as in EpiPens) or insulin when pharmaceutical firms dramatically increased the prices of old established drugs when market conditions allowed this action. The decision of how much to charge for the drug and whether it should require a prescription or be available over the counter is decided by panels of "experts" in corporate boardrooms after evaluating the safety and risk of abuse.

Not having any generic competition, new drugs are generally costly and are placed in a high tier or category for consumer co-pay as determined in insurance board rooms. Drug insurance can also limit the amount of medication they will permit with any single prescription, requiring repeated co-pays for each refill. Pharmaceutical manufacturers spend considerable money on advertising their newly released drugs directly to the consumer. The consumer is being lured into asking for this new drug, which requires a prescription. Is this new drug worth its added expense if the patient's condition is adequately managed with older, less expensive medicines? Is the more expensive product more effective, has fewer side effects, or is it easier to consume? The manufacturer spent considerable funds believing there was a favorable market for this product, but you may not require being in this market. It is your choice of what to do. You must discuss this with your doctor if you are uncertain.

Saving money on medications is a priority in the US. It is so recognized in Washington, D.C. Many consumers pick up their medications at a cheaper price during foreign travel or ask contacts abroad to send them cheaper products. To save money, some request higher doses that they can "cut in half" (thus saving both the effort of getting refills and the cost per pill). There also is an incentive to keep and take "outdated" pills rather than replace them with new pills. There is a "shelf life" to medications, and they can become outdated, but their efficacy does not suddenly cease as if falling off a cliff. Their potency is assured up to the date of expiration. Then begins a possible slow decline in potency, which makes them less effective but not dangerous. After a longer period (usually 1-2 years), they may decay to the point they become ineffective or dangerous.

You can ask the pharmacist about this concern. Some individuals try to maintain a "mini-pharmacy" at home consisting of antibiotics, hormones, or other common medicines to take in case of feeling "sick" or if their doctor orders them again. They also can share these unused medicines with their friends and neighbors when requested, saving friends the expense and effort of a doctor's office visit. Then some believe that "if a little amount of the medicine helped a little, a lot more of the medicine should help a lot more." This philosophy doesn't work any better with medicine than with cooking. It's best to stick to the prescribed instructions. A point to remember is that the cost of drugs is not always the same at all pharmacies. Shop around at different pharmacies in your community for their price (even with your drug insurance), and look into drug programs offering cut-rate pharmaceuticals.

The indiscriminate use of antibiotics is a major cause in encouraging antibiotic-resistant bacteria in the patient and community. This adds to the difficulty in healing infections with these resistant organisms. There is no antibiotic to which all germs are sensitive. Bacteria that are resistant to an antibiotic in their environment blossom, having less competition for food and space from sensitive bacteria that are eliminated. Taking an ineffective antibiotic only serves to run the risk of an allergic reaction and encourages more resistant bacteria in the community. The danger can escalate to a point where other patients acquire severe bacterial infections with organisms for which no antibiotics are effective. Taking the wrong antibiotic for the incorrect diagnosis can also cause unnecessary fungal and severe intestinal infections in the treated patient. The unneeded antibiotic eliminates the "useful" normal flora that inhabits everyone's intestines, opening an opportunity for competitive and "opportunistic" bacterial replacement by less beneficial and dangerous organisms. Antibiotic-induced diarrhea and colitis are common consequences.

Flushing unused or outdated medicines down the toilet is another no-no. Many prescription medicines, including antibiotics and hormones, end up in streams or waters with living fish or plants, entering our food chain while affecting the regional biosphere. This is becoming an increasing public health problem. Most communities collect old medicines for appropriate disposal.

Then, there is the problem of older people opening their pill bottles. Unless specifically instructed otherwise, the pharmacist will most likely dispense medications in a "childproof" container that is extremely difficult for most elderly people to open. The consequence of this protective cap is that many elderly do not securely close the lids of their medicine bottles, and pills spill out - everywhere. Loose pills are often found in handbags, pockets, and pouches. Patients frequently find such loose pills, collect them, and show them to the doctor or assistant, requesting that they identify and match them with the appropriate prescription and bottle.

Others may guess what they appear to be and take them in error. Older patients should ask the pharmacist if the medicines could be dispensed in a more easily opened container. Not only will this avoid a lot of frustration, but it will also reduce the risk of taking the wrong medication and avoid knife injuries sustained when trying to open the pill bottle.

There is also a significant risk of "polypharmacy" in the elderly. Drug interactions are tested between several commonly used drugs. Still, when a person takes more than 3 or 4 different medicines, there is a great likelihood that this combination has never been adequately investigated. With two medicines (A and B), toxicities may develop to A, B, and AB. With three medicines (A, B, and C) reactions can occur to A, B, C, AB, BC, AC, and ABC. As the number of medicines taken increases, potential interactions increase exponentially. There then develops an increasing risk of unexpected drug interactions drugs that interfere with one another in an unspecified way. Furthermore, the more medications a person takes with different time and interval schedules, the greater the risk for noncompliance - too confusing and frustrating.

Most patients take their medications regularly and as directed, but some intentionally refrain from taking the medicines on the day of the doctor's appointment. For example, taking a diuretic on the day when traveling to the doctor in a not-toilet-friendly environment can lead to an embarrassing situation. Patients may also hold off on taking their medicines on the day of the visit due to the erroneous belief that their doctor may want to do blood tests and that the medication may interfere with test results. They then may claim to be taking the medicines regularly (which they are) but do not mention they omitted taking the medicine that day. The doctor may then mistakenly think the medications are not as effective as expected and increase the dose or change the medication, not knowing the patient has not taken the medication for 24 hours. The patient should always tell the provider if they had not taken the medications that day, and doctors should always ask that critical question.

Then, there is the issue of the medication's name and appearance. Each medication has three names: a chemical name, a brand name, and a generic name. Medicines from abroad may have their brand and generic names in different languages. The public is often confused about the names. It is not by accident that generic names are hard to pronounce (and therefore harder to remember) and are generally 3 to 4 syllables long.

In contrast, brand names are shorter and easier to remember. Pharmaceutical companies want consumers to remember and refer to their brand products and not use competitive generic medications. Patients must learn the names of the medicines they take. This is not always easy because the names may not be familiar, and generic names are tough to pronounce. It is worth expending the time and effort to learn and practice pronouncing the names, strengths, and schedules of each of your medicines. Doctors (and nurses) will always ask you which drugs you are taking, and if you respond with a blank stare, it looks terrible and labels you as a problem patient. Writing down and keeping a list of medications with their details on your person is helpful when visiting doctors, traveling, or during emergency visits to a hospital.

Unlike brand-named products, generic drugs are not required to mimic the branded medication in shape or color. To get FDA approval for a generic, the generic must be within 10-15% efficacy of the brand (this small alteration in efficacy usually makes little difference). Any change in the appearance of a new generic compared to what they had been taking can disturb the consumer. They will wonder if the pharmacist had given them the wrong medicine in a refill, even if the generic names are the same.

Changes in medicines also happen when people are admitted to a hospital. Unlike a community pharmacy, the hospital pharmacy does not carry all the medications individuals might take at home. Hospitals will stock representative medications of important pharmaceutical groups. By limiting which medications of any particular class or purpose they will carry, they can negotiate prices with their distributors in a way much more to their advantage. "Do you want us to purchase your drug, or should we stock your competitor's drug?" "They have similar actions and benefits, but the costs are different." "Do you want to be competitive?" This, too, leads to some patient confusion when, in the hospital, the patient is not given the same exact medicines they had been taking at home. And because it is a different medication, doses may differ, but the effects should be the same. As mentioned above, some disorders are dependent on the diet, activity, and stress the patient is encountering. Hospitals will alter the patient's medications to meet the patient's immediate needs. After hospital discharge, the individual may need (with the help of their doctor) to readjust their medications back to what they took before hospitalization.

Similarly to hospital pharmacies, drug plans with their pharmaceutical insurance can be selective in which medications they will support and pay for. Aside from tier designation, they also eliminate coverage for many prescribed medications. Drug plans naturally prefer to choose medications which have been discounted by the manufacturer to win their endorsement. Manufacturers of competing products are thus encouraged to discount their medications. When doctors write prescriptions, they may not know the medication they order may not be covered in the patient's drug plan. Paying out-of-pocket for that medicine is very expensive. The consumer is caught in the middle of a medicine price competition war that they know nothing about. The patient can then ask the prescriber if they would endorse a medicine which is covered in their drug plan, (a generic or a similar product). For most pharmaceutical needs, there are many medications available (although they all have some differences). Alternatively, patents can go to cut-rate pharmacies or use a cut rate offering through companies like "Single Care" or "Good Rx"). Alternatively, they may try to get these medicines from abroad. They should shop around for getting the most affordable price. This behavior can also have ripple effects on how insurance companies choose their coverage and pharmaceutical companies determine their pricing.

Frequently, medications are changed before the patient's supply has been exhausted, and the patient is left with a variety of drugs in their home that they no longer take. These should be put into a separate location and labeled "inactive." **Never** keep these alongside "active" drugs - the drugs you regularly take. If a medical emergency occurs and EMS is called, they are trained to collect all the medications they find and bring them to the Emergency Department with the patient. Since the individual may not be able to identify which drugs they take or do not take, the assumption is that all the accompanying medicines are being taken in the manner prescribed and indicated on the bottle label. The drugs will be administered by hospital staff as written.

Drug allergies are another source of confusion. Every medication has "inactive" ingredients in addition to the marquis "active" ingredient. These are fillers, binders, coloring compounds, and preservatives, often comprising the bulk of the pill or capsule. Allergic reactions can occur to any ingredient; therefore, identifying the agent responsible for an adverse reaction or allergy can be difficult. Most people will blame it on the labeled medication and carry this "allergic" label with them for the rest of their lives. Generic drugs are not required to use the same "inactive" ingredients as the brand product, and an allergy to an additive can lead to unwanted fears and avoidance. This is mainly a problem with allergies to the coloring compounds.

For many patients, just taking their medications as prescribed can be difficult. Some labels state the medication should be taken with food, others with water only and not any other medication. Some medicines are to be taken at night or bedtime, while others are first thing in the morning. Some every 6 or 8 hours, and others twice or three times a day. It becomes almost impossible for the average patient, taking multiple medications, to follow all these directions as prescribed. This problem is compounded when a person is seeing several physicians. Each physician prescribes medicines independently but considers what other medicines the patient is taking, but may not consider the confusing time schedules. This makes the patient's prescription orders more complicated and confusing. Taking medicines as directed can become the main focus of the day, and the individual can spend their entire day looking at the clock and taking their medicines as told. That is not what living is supposed to be. Most people just take the medicines at their convenience, disregarding the actual directions. This works for most disorders, but timing may be critical for some (such as those for Parkinson's disease). If the regimen becomes too complicated, the patient should talk to the prescribing individual about simplifying the schedule and if all their medicines are necessary. Compromises may have to be made. Doctors may also be unfamiliar with the cost of the various medicines. Patients should not be embarrassed about asking whether there are cheaper versions of the medicines that might have the same benefit.

Reading all the warnings about any medicine can be alarming. Pharmacy inserts and internet sites list all the potential problems reported in people taking the medicine (severe or common). This protects the company from liability if there is an undesired side effect. The FDA requires listing adverse reactions if they occur more frequently than 1-3 percent of the time (this also means it may not happen 97 percent of the time). Some of these "adverse" reactions are clearly due to the medication effect (too potent or too high a dose), but sometimes causality is not apparent. An individual who reads these theoretical risks and worries about the medicine's safety will probably be afraid to take any medicine; they should discuss their concerns with their doctor. Adverse effects can occur with taking any medicine, even placebos. An anxious patient may sense that he or she has all the symptoms and complaints listed as possible problems associated with the medicine and be afraid to take anything. Many common complaints occur even when not taking medicine, giving less certainty about their cause. However, an adverse reaction to a medicine is common in patients taking multiple medications.

So, how does one determine whether a medicine is helpful or harmful? This is a common question. Your doctor can draft a plan of slowly eliminating a questionable drug to observe how you respond, shift the time of administration to see if that changes the time of symptom occurrence, or stop those suspected medicines that can be stopped abruptly. Patients should not do this alone, as some drugs require slow weaning before stopping. Resolving this issue requires a cooperative effort of the patient and doctor. This point needs emphasis. Medications that "block" or interfere with normal bodily function may result in your body adapting to this block. A sudden cessation of the blocker may bring on a severe life-threatening reaction. It is analogous to driving a car with one foot on the gas and one on the brake. The "blocking" drug is like a brake trying to reduce the effects of a function that is too active.

Suddenly stopping the medication is like suddenly taking your foot off the brake.

Taking over-the-counter medicines is also not without risk. Any chemicals and nonprescription medicines you take should be discussed with your doctor to keep your doctor informed and your drug records accurate. Such is true with nonproprietary supplements and vitamins. Very little in life is risk-free, and consuming excessive amounts of vitamins and minerals (primarily vitamins A, D, E, and Calcium) can have dire consequences. Compounds that are "natural" does not mean they are safe. There are a lot of natural poisons out there. Conversely, taking "not approved" medicines does not mean they are dangerous. This only means that insufficient information about medication use for a particular illness has been given to the FDA for approval. "Off-label" usage only means insufficient testing for approval of use to treat that disorder. It does not mean it cannot be tried for the indication the doctor is addressing.

Reviewing one's medications with the doctor at each visit is helpful. Sometimes, patients are still taking medications that the doctor believes were discontinued long ago; other times, new prescriptions were never filled while the records show the medicine was prescribed; and other times, your doctor was never aware another caregiver had given you a new prescription which you are taking.

Occasionally, patients accept the recommendations, advice, and medications offered by their friends and neighbors who have had similar complaints. It seems they trust suggestions from trusted friends and relatives more than those from a new doctor who has not yet earned their confidence. Patients may be too embarrassed to reveal this critical detail to their doctor.

Patients should pack a list of their medicines (preferably with doses and schedules) if traveling. Even with language barriers, most doctors abroad will understand these medications by their names, dosages, and schedules.

Chapter 6
CHOICES DURING EMERGENCIES

Emergencies are not what they used to be - it's best to be prepared

Emergencies can and do happen to everyone. And when they happen, people are often unprepared and unsure of what to do. In the past, they called their trusted doctor to seek help and get immediate advice. But, as we know, times have changed, and the doctor's role in emergencies is not as it had been. The patient might not even know a trusted doctor they can call. Doctors now rarely make home visits or call ambulances to take patients to emergency rooms (often called Emergency Departments or EDs). Now, patients must make their own decisions, usually on the advice of some trusted family authority. We all recognize that emergency rooms are the most expensive and complex areas to visit in a hospital and places we all want to avoid. Medical emergencies can occur anytime: day, night, weekend, or holiday.

Without advance notice, emergency rooms must be ready to manage whatever kind of emergency develops in their community and comes through their doors. This can result from a building collapse, a 4-alarm fire, an act of terrorism or mass shooting, a train crash, or exposure to toxins in a school. People arrive at all hours with chest pain or difficulty breathing. A parent carries in a terrified toddler who managed to stick something up their nose that got stuck. Emergency Departments must maintain an operating staff of professionals 24 hours a day, seven days a week, regardless of whether only one patient arrives or if there are hundreds of patients. Anything can happen at any time, and emergency rooms need to be prepared to respond to any imaginable disaster.

Busy emergency rooms can resemble a chaotic battlefield. There can be loud crying and screaming from infants and adults. Staff may be seen rushing about with portable oxygen, intravenous pumps, and vital-sign monitors. There is a continued need for changing linens and cleaning, as severely ill patients may be bleeding, vomiting, voiding, and generally soiling their beds. Nurses, Aides, and attendants may be seen carrying soiled or fresh linens, mops, and waste containers. Foul odors may permeate the air. Patients are lying on gurneys (rolling stretchers), placed wherever there is available space, and they can be vomiting, bleeding, or screaming in pain. Family members often run frantically around, trying desperately to find anyone to talk with who can provide information about their loved one's status. It's natural to expect the family to be concerned and crave the latest information about the patient's condition. Unlike the busy and often overworked staff, the family has only one individual about whom they are vitally concerned. The Emergency Department is not like a doctor's waiting room or office. It is not a calming or relaxing environment.

To maintain this capability, emergency rooms must have staff onsite to perform all necessary testing, take and interpret any X-rays, EKGs, and CT scans required, perform resuscitation, provide wound care, accomplish simple orthopedic surgeries, manage psychiatric emergencies, and be able to offer isolation facilities for the management of patients with potential infectious danger to the public. They must be equipped to handle emergencies in infants and the aged. They also require a rapid response network to urgently summon additional specialized staff needed at any time of day or night should the need arise. Occasionally, as occurred during the Covid crisis, emergency rooms can become overwhelmed and must refer patients to neighboring facilities. Emergency rooms keep in contact to check each other's bed status.

Usually, emergency rooms fill up their prepared spaces, with all the built-in needed equipment (monitors, oxygen, suction) firsr, then the hallways. When these are filled, patients are placed in any available storeroom or open space before referring them elsewhere.

In urban hospital emergency departments, it can become hectic and frantic. Many different languages may be heard, a polyglot. Foreign visitors to the US often use emergency rooms for unexpected medical problems, as they have no local doctor they know of to call. They may bring interpreters to assist the staff and patients in communication. Patients, families, and visitors can become frantic, demanding, and behaving irrationally. Onsite hospital security is always available and visible, ready to escort disruptive individuals out of the ED. Social workers frequent the area to assist with common and uncommon social issues: contacting family, arranging transportation, facilitating referrals and transfers, and helping with the needs of the distressed patient. Frequently, insurance coverage and approval issues are needed to resolve payment concerns. Social workers are instrumental in helping patients with their financial and coverage conflicts. However, as stated before, most problems involve contacting companies that follow a 9-5 weekday schedule, unlike the ED's 24-hour, 7-day-a-week schedule. Emergency room staff must restrict traffic in and out of the ED to allow the medical team to function and manage all their patients without interference despite the frequent congestion. A head nurse usually manages the chaos and maintains a sense of order and coordination of services. If visitors could remove themselves from the activity and just observe the chaos from an objective vantage, they would see that, despite the appearance of chaos, there is an order and a pattern to the workings of the ED. It is a complex symphony (sometimes a bit atonal) of movement and activity.

Emergency medicine is now a board-certified specialty for qualified doctors with advanced training in life support, surgery, psychiatry, pediatric emergencies, toxicology, and cardiopulmonary crises. ED doctors are salaried and work 8-hour shifts.

The ED doctors 'relationship with the patient is acute and brief (generally less than 24 hours). Rarely is there any follow-up. Patients are treated and discharged or admitted to the hospital for further care after stabilization; some critical patients may expire. Most EDs try to "move patients along." They need open spaces for any new patient arrivals and try to keep patients in the ED for less than 24 hours. However, if a patient needs admission and no beds are available in the hospital, the patient must remain in the ED until such a bed can be found. At times, such waiting can last more than a day. The patient's care may then be transferred to the hospital floor staff, where the assigned care team comes down to the ED to manage the patient. Hospital beds in regular rooms are far more comfortable than gurneys in the ED; every patient wants to transfer to a standard and quiet room, and the patient and family will keep inquiring about when the patient will be moved to a regular hospital bed.

Staff in the ED often practice *triage* when crises occur, and the staff is overwhelmed (*triage* is a French term dating from the Napoleonic battlefield practice). In triage, patients are separated into one of three categories according to their perceived urgency for medical attention: 1) a patient who is considered not critically ill and attention can be postponed or be given only cursory and limited care; 2) a patient who is considered in need of some immediate attention and will then be able to leave or help others, and 3) those so ill they will probably not survive or will take enormous amounts of time and attention to manage. With staff shortage, group 2 patients will be given priority, while group 3 patients will be placed to the side.

The cost of running the Emergency room is very high, and salaries for the large staff are huge by any standard. Insurance will pay only for their subscribers, so ED costs will continue even when no patients arrive and no income materializes. To support a functioning ED, insurance payments are much higher than at a medical office to compensate for staff salaries when no patients are seen. But, even with patients, running an emergency room is expensive and can be a financial loss to the hospital.

The average patient is in the emergency room for hours. They will likely need to be fed a meal and be seen by multiple caregivers. This then leads to a problem when people with minor infections or complaints choose to go to an ED at night, on weekends, or on holidays for expediency or convenience, when their regular doctor is not in his or her medical office, and when the telephone response says "Go to the Emergency Room."

Someone coming in with a runny nose competes for attention with true emergencies, and no one can be ignored. As stated, this is the most expensive form of medical care available, and valuable time and attention should not be siphoned away from genuine emergencies. Emergency rooms are not walk-in clinics. This is why Urgent Care centers have been created. They have defined hours of operation and require fewer resources. The costs are much less than in an ED, but they are not open 24/7.

In the past, when doctors made house calls regularly, the referral to an Emergency room was made only after the patient was seen and examined during a house call in their home. In making the home visit, the doctor was limited in what they could easily carry with them. No significant testing could be done. After a brief examination, an ambulance could be called. Today, patients dial

"911" for an emergency. In true medical emergencies, such as a patient with a stroke or heart attack, time may be of the essence. Similarly, with chest or head wounds, care cannot be delayed. Emergency treatment may be delayed for hours if the patient waits for the home visit. Today, many doctors will listen to the patient's complaint by phone (if phone contact can be achieved) and advise the patient appropriately. The doctor will often call the hospital to alert them to the patient's impending arrival, and some doctors will meet the patient in the ED.

Advanced planning is extremely helpful in emergency situations. Patients should discuss with their families a plan for emergency response before the emergency occurs. Patients often have a favorite hospital to which they would prefer their care (in emergencies and for hospitalization). That chosen hospital is probably accepted in the patient's medical network. However, a "911" call triggers a visit by an ambulance with its EMT staff. They are instructed to take the patient to the closest Emergency Room if they suspect or worry the patient is unstable. Consideration of the patient's insurance acceptability is not their concern. This avoids delays in transport. However, the closest hospital may not be the first choice for the patient, the patient's family, or the insurance carrier. Nonetheless, the ambulance takes them to the nearest open ED if they assess the patient's condition as precarious. If the patient needs hospital admission, it will be to the hospital associated with that ED and not to their preferred hospital with their preferred medical or surgical staff. Once accepted by an ED, transfer to a different ED is not an option. EDs do not transfer patients to other EDs. If the patient is stable and wants to transfer to another facility, the only mechanism available is to demand discharge against medical advice (or AMA) and arrange transportation to the preferred hospital, hoping a bed is available and the doctors there will accept the patient for admission. Alternatively, the patient does not call 911 but instead calls a private ambulance, which will take them to whichever emergency room and hospital they designate. Medical insurance generally pays for this. This choice of who to call in an emergency will depend on an assessment of the emergency and the status of the patient (assuming the nearest hospital is not the preferred one). The time difference between going to one hospital and another depends on distance and traffic. Time should not be wasted discussing options and looking up telephone numbers for ambulance services, hospitals, and telephone operators. Occasionally, after receiving telephone busy signals or being in a panic, the family shoves the patient into their car and rushes them to the nearest hospital ED. A call to the local police precinct might even afford a police escort to avoid traffic lights. An advanced plan can be critical and should be worked out with the family and the family doctor. In preparing a plan for emergencies, individuals should know in advance which ED is the closest to their home, whether the associated hospital is covered in their medical plan, and if they would choose to be taken to that hospital. They should have available the telephone number(s) of private ambulance service(s) to call if there is another facility they would prefer, recognizing the consequences of their decisions. An emergency is not the time to start thinking about what to do. In an emergency, people may not be as level-headed and capable of thinking as clearly as they would when they are not harried and are more reflective.

In the ED, the family doctor can provide needed medical information if no savvy family member accompanies the patient in the ambulance. If possible, this can also be done by phone contact. Otherwise, having the family doctor visit the patient is little more than just having another visitor. It is purely a social call on "off hours," for which the doctor will receive no compensation. The family doctor is not likely to be authorized to treat patients in the

ED or to have been trained in Emergency medicine. They cannot order any tests or treatments. After making a few comments about the patient's background and expressing his or her thoughts concerning the problem, the doctor becomes just another visitor, blocking access to other patients and standing in the way of the bustling staff. It may be very reassuring to the patient and the accompanying family to see the family doctor at this frightening and uncertain moment, but this may be the only benefit of the family doctor being there. On the other hand, the staff may be overwhelmed with other critical patients and will probably resent intrusions on their time by extraneous, unrequested, and unnecessary interruptions. They also don't need more people standing around their patients. A quick assessment of what is happening in the ED will guide the family and visiting doctor regarding how much help or hindrance their presence is making.

Chapter 7
SURVIVING HOSPITALIZATION

When total strangers control your life

Hospitals can be dangerous places, particularly for elderly patients. Hospital stays are not like those in the past. Understanding today's hospitals and routines is the first step towards a satisfactory hospital stay. A better understanding may also help the patient's (and the patient's family's) composure and sanity and help reduce potential errors in care. Hospitals have become complex institutions and businesses, with more personnel involved in many more patient services than ever before.

Physicians no longer run hospitals. Business executives now do and are under the same pressures experienced by executives of any large business or corporation (meet your expenses or get fired and go bankrupt). Hospital executives' salaries must be competitive with those of other companies. With modern technological advances and increases in needed personnel, the cost of operating the facility has increased dramatically. These costs eventually get passed on to the patient and the insurance companies.

A recent and growing trend around the country is the purchase of hospitals, medical practices, EDs, and Home Care agencies by private equity companies. New management makes new rules at their discretion. Continuation of any existing policies in care and costs are no longer assured. Any expectations of the patient based on past experiences may be unrealized. Whether such purchases are funded by private capital investors or with bank loans, increased revenue will be needed from the purchased entity to cover the cost of acquisition and any accumulating interest on the principal. Purchased facilities are immediately saddled with significant financial burdens, even those that previously had been financially secure. Aside from requiring payment of interest on loans and monetary rewards to the investors, the venture capital executive officers demand a high salary.

The medical facility has become fully corporatized. How will these private equity groups realize a profitable return on their investment? Financial pressure on the purchased medical facilities encourages a reduction in expenditures and increased fees wherever possible. The counterargument for the venture capital group claims the new medical corporation brings a much-needed infusion of money for expansion and improvements. While this may be true in some instances, venture capital groups are not choosing to buy the less profitable medical facilities that sorely need the new money; they prefer the more successful ones. This is where the prospect of greater profit lies.

Disturbingly, a strong profit motive may compete with and supersede sound clinical judgment. Doctors are pressured to reduce expenses and increase profits by their clinical decisions, while nursing and office staff are let go to save salaries. Many concerned doctors and other staff members have voluntarily left these facilities, upset by managerial changes. These positions are then offered to less experienced personnel who are more than willing to accept the new terms of employment. Moreover, when patient-care medical facilities are purchased by venture capital groups that have also purchased nursing homes, rehabilitation facilities, home nursing agencies, laboratories, radiology groups, etc., it is appropriate to question the motivation behind any referrals to these facilities. The short and long-term effects of these profit-incentivized changes in medical management should be of great concern to the public and are currently under intense scrutiny. Recent studies suggest a deterioration in the quality of care when facilities are purchased by private equity firms.

Furthermore, for the hospitalized patient, the more complex the medical problem and the more people involved in patient care, the greater the opportunity for mistakes. Expect that things will not be as they were in the past, but try to partner the best you can with your hospital team (don't just be a patient or a passive object to be manipulated). Getting better is easier if everyone involved in your care (you and the treating staff) are on the same page and communicating effectively. Being helpful and assistive in your care can be to your benefit. Begin by asking anyone caring for you their names and functions. This makes your interactions more personal and human. Addressing the staff by their name and title emphasizes that you both are human, and changes the relationship. Jot down their names for reference, or ask them for their names again if you forget.

Hospitals differ in type and in their priorities. When hospitalized, you should know what kind of hospital you are hospitalized in. There are public or government hospitals, private for-profit hospitals, voluntary hospitals, teaching hospitals, university hospitals, and specialty hospitals. City, county, state, or federal administrations fund and manage public hospitals. All staff (including the doctors) are salaried. The Veterans Administration is a known example, but there are prison hospitals, military hospitals, native American hospitals, and health services for all government agencies that fall under this umbrella. They depend on government subsidies and grants to exist and for politicians to appreciate their service and provide funding. Private hospitals are privately run for profit and may be managed by health-related corporations, investors, or private groups. They depend on payment for services from health insurance companies, patients, donations, and/or corporate support. Voluntary hospitals are not-for-profit hospitals where their priority is patient care. Staff in these hospitals (including hospitalist doctors) are also salaried.

Teaching and university hospitals are affiliated with a teaching institution, such as a medical school and university.

There are some hospital practices and agendas you should know and understand. University-affiliated hospitals are primarily concerned with the education and training of students, along with research. These are their priorities that compete with patient care. Patients may feel more secure at a premier university medical center, but they are cared for by students and house staff under teaching attending supervision. Except in smaller, mostly rural hospitals, patient care is managed by hospitalists. Almost all hospitals have patient liaisons and advocates readily available to help patients with problems during their hospital stay. One needs only to ask for their assistance. Their services are free. Social workers on staff are also mandated, at no cost, to assist the patient. They help patients and their families cope with hospital and post-discharge care issues. Understanding the type of hospital and needs of the institution in which you are a patient can help you better understand your situation and the facility's priorities.

If confused or upset, the first key is to ask questions, mainly if there are things you don't understand or think something is being done inappropriately. But direct your questions and speak to the appropriate person. Your questions should be framed in a thoughtful and meaningful way rather than an accusatory manner that will generate a defensive response. Next, ask a family advocate or surrogate to see you regularly. Being a patient, you most likely will be confined to a bed with limited awareness of what is happening around you. You will also be preoccupied with testing, procedures, therapies, and people asking you multiple seemingly repetitive questions. You need someone who knows you, cares about you personally, and can supply hospital staff with information that the hospital records may not contain. You need someone who can observe what is happening in the hospital outside of your room and evaluate your situation objectively in a fresh, unbiased manner. In the hospital, there is a tendency to treat patients as diseases, chart numbers, or "cases." The presence of your personal advocate reminds hospital staff you are a real person who has outside influence and contacts while keeping tabs on your status. It tells the staff their behavior is being noticed and hopefully appreciated. An occasional box of cookies or chocolate given to the staff physically demonstrates your gratitude. Your advocate also brings a bit of the outside world to you and keeps you oriented and informed of relevant news and what is happening with your family and contacts.

Further, if there is a conflict, your advocate (being more mobile than you) is better positioned to present your difficulties and argue for your rights. If you have questions or concerns, your advocate can help. Lastly, remember that different individuals in your care may have other agendas. Your agenda, and that of your doctor and advocate, is to get you healed and discharged in a better condition than when you were admitted. The hospital's agenda is to care for multiple patients, have available beds for new admissions, and remain financially solvent. In a teaching hospital, students and doctors in training may see you as a vehicle to learn more about your disorder; the resident or fellow specializing in a particular specialty wants to see every patient in that hospital with that disorder to gain more experience in as short a period as possible. An insurance representative wants to see if there is a valid reason for your admission. A research assistant sees you as an item in a study to prove a hypothesis. Usually, you can identify the role of the person addressing you by what their interest is and how they interact and approach you. Most may want to do their job and go home, but they are all human and wish you well. Your interaction with them depends on the nature of their job description. If you understand their intentions, you can interact with them in a more constructive manner.

The advocate above is a person you choose, know, and trust. Typically, it is a family member. However, there is another advocate in the hospital. Hospitals employ patient advocates to help patients with issues related to their care. Like a social worker, this advocate is available at your request to resolve difficulties you may be having with the staff or administration. You can complain to the nurse if you object to the discharge conditions and are dissatisfied with your room or any other hospital service. If it is still unresolved, you may engage the assistance of the hospital social worker and then advocate. You have rights as a patient and as a citizen. Another source for resolving larger insurance or hospital action issues is your city, county, or state political representatives. For large major issues, you can bring your complaint to your congressman or senator. Their primary role is to represent your interests in government. Most corporations make you feel like an insignificant item they can manipulate. When dealing with large, organized facilities, it is easy to feel unimportant or helpless. Older people grew up at a time when people said, "You can't fight city hall!" But today, you can. It is your choice. You can seek change and obtain redress depending on your hurt and dissatisfaction. Fighting city hall is time-consuming and requires effort, but you may be surprised at how much support and power you can muster.

Many patients are disturbed by how their medical care seems to unfold. Your carefully selected family physician is not in charge. Your care has been assigned to a hospitalist, not of your choosing. Someone you probably have never yet met and who has no familiarity with you or your case. And this is at a time when you are hospitalized, most ill, and when your life may be at risk. It is then when total strangers are making all the critical decisions. After admission to the hospital, a nurse usually visits you first and asks you many questions. This will be followed by a young doctor, who will likely ask you the same questions but add more questions (going into greater depth and detail to understand your problems). Later, you will meet your hospitalist, who will be an attending licensed physician and who will be managing your case. And the hospitalist will ask you the same questions. All this repetitive questioning leaves you exhausted and usually upset. You are ill, tired, maybe in pain, and have just been admitted after many hours of waiting (in transit or in an Emergency Room). You want to rest or sleep and be left alone, not be interviewed with the same questions over and over again. Nature wants every sick or injured being to seek a safe location, shelter themselves, and not expose themselves to predators. We want the same when not feeling well. You may ask, "Why don't they just ask for your answers from the previous individual who questioned you and leave you in peace, huddled under a blanket?" But repetitive questioning has its value. With repeated questioning, you may recall more details, become more aware of what is important and irrelevant in your narrative, and become a better historian. The last person questioning you frequently gets the most important history; this is usually the person with the most responsibility for your care.

Ask your hospitalist how you might reach her or him if **needed** (a pager or mobile number). The word "needed" is essential since phone calls interrupt what your doctor is doing at the time of your call. Your call should not be for a long discussion but for a quick answer to a specific question or to report a problem. You can mention this possibility to your hospitalist beforehand. Use common sense. Orders for testing procedures or discharges are issued by your attending physician. Therefore, it is not unreasonable to inquire about the best means to reach the doctor directly without going through or waiting hours to see the unit nurse. In teaching hospitals, you may also have students (nursing and medical) and doctors-in-training (what had been called "interns" and "residents" and are now called PGY-1, 2, or 3, meaning post-graduation year 1, 2, or 3). Doctors in specialty training (fellowship) may also see you if your illness is of particular concern and interest to them.

Other frequently annoying details of hospital stays concern daily weights, annoying beeping sounds and alarms going off, noisy neighbors, and sleep interruptions with seemingly unnecessary trivial issues. Your rest or sleep may also be disturbed by new hospital staff beginning their 8-hour shift and checking in on your condition. Hospitals are not hotels and are structured for efficient delivery of needed care; they are not prioritized for patient comfort (although this is considered). Patient comfort is even more compromised in a double room or multi-bed area. An Intensive Care Unit (ICU) is the space least designed for patient comfort. Understand also that if you are confined to bed, you have become totally dependent upon others for all your needs, such as bed pans, urinals, fresh linen, food, drink, etc. Indeed, you have lost all your independence and have essentially been infantilized. You may feel you have lost your identity and have become the number on your wristband. You may sense you have become a commodity, no longer a person. Although wristband numbers have reduced the number of procedural errors when misidentifying patients (particularly those whose names are unfamiliar or difficult to pronounce for most Americans) by staff administering medications or sending patients for procedures, this form of identification has its drawbacks. It can be a reminder of how Nazis stenciled tattoo numbers on the arms of inmates at Auschwitz death camp. Its purpose there was to erase the human identity of the individual. We now have other means of identification that can be used and which retain a more human element. Having visitors and advocates visiting you keeps your humanity evident to all.

Unless you have been labeled as a "VIP," your identity, dignity, and comfort are relegated to minimal importance. Despite the expressed concern and goal for first-rate medical care for all citizens, we recognize that we already have multiple levels of care in quality and availability as determined by your residence, celebrity, and position in society. No one doubts that leading government officials get priority care as compared to the masses. Similarly, major donors to hospitals and other medical facilities expect and usually get faster, superior attention and greater undisputed health benefits.

Depending upon the activity in your hospital unit, hospital staff may be preoccupied with other hospital matters and not be able to respond quickly to your requests. You can't call for room service as in a hotel. The hospital policy regarding patient comfort, services, and respect may be one thing, but these aspects often depend on a single night nurse or aide assigned to you and who has had a good or bad day.

As stated above, hospitals are not hotels but rather are dangerous places. They are growth centers for bacteria with resistance to many antibiotics, making their eradication difficult. Close physical contact and exposure to staff and patients with various transmissible diseases increases your chances of developing transmissible hospital-related infections. Having your intact skin and other natural body defenses violated by invasive catheters, needles, and procedures bypasses many normally protective bodily functions. You probably will be given new medications - ones to which no one yet knows how your body will react. You have exchanged your secure home environment for a foreign one replete with threats of new, unanticipated problems.

Effective interaction with hospital personnel is a critical aspect of successful hospitalization. Realize that, even with the best intentions, hospital personnel see the older patient differently than does the family. Staff do not know who you are; they interact with you as they see you. Your family sees you in a loving and understanding way and as a unique individual. Everyone should be working on the same page with the same goal: getting you better and being able to go home with the admitting problem resolved. Showing the staff some appreciation for their labor can win some favors. Knowing there are outside people invested in the care of the patient and noticing how well the patient is being attended to also has a beneficial effect. With poor communication and different agendas, conflicts can occur. In a conflict, ranting and screaming at hospital personnel is very counterproductive.

Hospitals are paid by insurance companies based on the patient's diagnosis at the time of discharge, not by accounting for actual costs. There are adjustments based on outlying or complicating factors. This means that hospitals will receive the same remuneration for any specific illness or diagnosis, predetermined by their location and expected operating costs, and not by the number of days the patient spends in the hospital or actual costs of care delivery, testing, or procedures. This policy leads to an emphasis on "length of stay" for all hospital patients. Staff are urged to discharge patients as quickly as possible. Keeping a patient in the hospital for extended days loses income. That patient's bed could be filled by another patient whose insurance will pay for the hospital care. No added income is expected by keeping the patient in the hospital for more than 24 hours. This encourages early discharge as long as it is safe and does not endanger the patient's life. To expedite care, patients may be subjected to many investigative or treatment procedures on the same day, weekends not exempted. This condenses the procedures into the shortest possible time and shortens hospital stay. Many older patients object to this routine, as they tire easily, and being taken for frequent testing or treatments is exhausting. They may voice their complaint, arguing they are not sacks of potatoes that can be moved about indiscriminately and without consideration.

They may refuse to accede to the order, demanding more time for rest. To the hospital, this noncompliance delays discharge.

Focusing on a patient's hospital length-of-stay results in the common scenario of the patient and the family questioning why the patient is being discharged or transferred to another institution when they are still ill and recovering. "Does the hospital have no consideration for what this means to the family and patient? Where is their compassion?" If discharged home, someone there will need to pick up where the hospital left off if a patient has not fully recovered. The primary reason, of course, is money, and money concerns override everything else! Length of stay correlates inversely with income. However, early discharge has some benefits for the patient, as acute care hospitals are dangerous places that are not conducive to rest and recovery. In addition, prolonged hospitalizations often lead some patients to develop a psychological dependency on institutional care. They can become terrified at leaving the hospital's security (with its supportive staff) for the care uncertainties at home.

The fees to the hospital are also determined by the type of care being administered: acute care, chronic care, rehabilitative care, etc. When insurance companies determine an acute-care hospital is not filling the days of care with actively needed treatment, the hospital will not be paid for acute care. Payment for these days will be carved out. Lower fees are paid for subacute, chronic, and rehabilitative care in such designated facilities. This demonstrates that the patient's interests compete with the financial concerns of the facility and the insurance corporation.

Many patients become disoriented and confused in the hospital. An institutional policy of moving patients to different rooms on different floors with different staff depending on the needs and availability of services can be very disorienting and dangerous to patients already experiencing some confusion. Disturbing sleep and having procedures performed at night also have a negative effect on orientation. Having visits from family members to keep them oriented and reassured can prevent delusions and psychotic episodes in the patient. Some patients will try to remove catheters or climb out of bed. Others, who are terrified, will scream. All too frequently, patients get frightened and act in some bizarre way that triggers visits from psychiatrists and even prescriptions for tranquilizing medications or other restraining measures. This is mainly a problem in patients isolated in intensive care units.

The brain is an amazing organ; it is complicated in function but simple in its needs. Like a car engine, it needs fuel (glucose), an electric current (brain waves), and oxygen. When under stress or challenged, it can behave in an erratic way. A mature brain in a healthy individual keeps the person well-oriented and appropriate even under stressful situations. In extremes of youth and age, the brain often does not function at its best, and may malfunction under stress. And just as young children in twilight sleep can have hallucinations and see monsters, people with older brains are more at risk of having delusions, hallucinations, or episodes of disorientation with minimal provocation. Delusions are frequently seen with toxicities of infections, drugs (licit and illicit), high fevers, and altered blood metabolic components (they are called toxic-metabolic reactions). They can be seen if circulation problems reduce the oxygen and glucose reaching the brain. A delusion is a false belief about a reality. A delusion or hallucination is not indicative of dementia or psychosis. It is a temporary and acute phenomenon. But, hospital staff, not knowing the patient, may mistakenly believe this irrational behavior is the patient's norm. The delusion is not the sole problem; it is the symptom of altered metabolism and should be investigated and treated (looking for abnormalities in levels of glucose, thyroid hormone, or electrolytes). The family or advocate can help explain the acute nature of this behavior.

Not being aware of insurance payment policies, patients are often upset by hospital decisions. Similarly, hospitalized patients may ask why, if they have upcoming mammogram appointments or visits to a urologist, gastroenterologist, or another specialist, they can't be seen or have the procedure done while hospitalized. The appointment may even have been scheduled at that same institution on a day they are still hospitalized. Why must they be discharged, make a new appointment (which may not be easy), and return to the same facility? Wouldn't it be easier to do this while they are already at the facility? This sounds perfectly reasonable, but the answer again is payment and money. Whenever a patient or family finds hospital policies irrational and confusing, think of money. These are considered outpatient procedures paid by the insurance company following their payment policies. They will not pay these bills for an inpatient, even if the patient is handicapped and transportation is difficult. This policy may seem unnecessarily callous, but I'm sure they have decided it's more economical.

Chapter 8
HOME CARE

Is the comfort of home so comfortable and safe?

With large numbers of disabled individuals living at home, there is a need for both medical and personal care and assistance to be located in the home. Historically, this need was filled by families sharing the home with the disabled person. In today's world, families live apart, sometimes separated at great distances from each other, and most disabled persons do not wish to be a burden on or restrict the family's activities. If essentially homebound, disabled individuals relied on their doctor to make house calls for their medical care. In urban areas, many young doctors, or those who have less demand for their time and services, participate in programs like "doctors on call." These doctors make house calls when requested and generally accept health insurance. Their services are limited as to what instruments and medical records they can carry and utilize. They can examine the patient, obtain some history from the patient or family (if available), write prescriptions, order tests, refer the patient to more sophisticated medical facilities, and offer some needed guidance. The patient can then share any information obtained from these house calls with their regular medical doctor.

Many nursing agencies, including the Visiting Nurse Service, offer home nursing care. However, there are many nursing agencies, offering similar services and billing the patient's insurance for the payment of services. Some services include providing a social worker and offering assistance in obtaining a home health aide for help with personal care. As another alternative, a Case Manager can be employed whose responsibilities include accompanying the patient to doctors' offices, checking on home conditions (such as availability of food, need for cleaning, handling of personal finances, and other matters).

Such case managers (trained nurses or social workers) can summon vetted substitute aides if the primary aide cannot attend the patient. They can be the "eyes and ears" of family members living at a distance who worry about the status of their beloved relative. Many home care agencies arrange for case managers who can take on much of the burden that would typically fall on the family. They can also interact with the doctor caring for the patient to alert him or her about any problems they observe. Their involvement in caring for the disabled patient greatly relieves all concerned. Your insurance will likely not pay for a case manager, but you should ask.

For financial matters, most banks offer assistance in handling and paying bills, as directed by the patient or their agents. Family members are asked to wear many hats when caring for a debilitated patient - sometimes more than they can handle. They take on the everyday tasks the patient previously managed alone. They are the secretaries, chauffeurs, shoppers, advocates, money managers, advisors, and "Gal Fridays." Sometimes, all these responsibilities become too much of a burden for them. Although wanting to do everything for their loved one, they can't. They are human and have both physical and practical limits. Family members have their own lives and responsibilities. It is incumbent for families helping a disabled relative to recognize when they feel overwhelmed. If they crash from the strain, everyone will suffer. No one benefits. They must protect themselves and recognize they are not superhuman. It is easy for them to feel guilt in not being available to do "enough" or being unable to perform all the needed tasks. Most of these extra duties can be relegated to outside individuals who do these activities for a living. The only task that cannot be reassigned is remaining a loving and caring relative. This, still, is the most important function of a close family.

Most disabled, elderly, or chronically ill people prefer to live at home. It is more comfortable and convenient than being in a facility, such as in a residential apartment. There are pros and cons associated with every choice. Homes come with neighbors, nearby friends, and familiar environments. Institutions come with services, a community of peers, and professional oversight. I have had patients and family who have enjoyed being in a residential facility where they could socialize (and not just sit alone staring at a wall or TV), participate in book clubs, go on outings, and enjoy a varied tasty cuisine in the dining room. Others have loathed the environment of being confined to living with other people having severe disabilities and requiring assistance with all their personal needs. They want the independence to eat, sleep, and relax at their discretion, not on the schedules imposed at an institution.

People are all different, and diversity increases with aging. They differ in their wishes and needs. While staunchly protecting their dignity and independence, they may make foolish and impractical decisions. They choose where they are living and would want to choose where they will live in the future. However, they often need family guidance. Giving such guidance must be done in a way that does not embarrass or insult the older or disabled patient. You do not want to be regarded as an adversary by your loved one. You are family and working as a team, helping each other.

The reality is that as people age, they lose strength and endurance (that's what aging does). The older individual may become too feeble or incapacitated to perform all their normal daily routines without assistance. If there is no spouse or partner living with them, can they manage all their affairs without additional outside help? This may start with arranging a home cleaning service, paying bills, doing simple repairs, and shopping, but it can progress to helping with basic functions like washing, toileting, and feeding. Children may recognize the need for help long before the parent admits their frailty and accepts this reality. Daily needs do not decrease with aging, but the capacity to accomplish the tasks does decrease. Eventually, we all will need help if we live long enough. Needing additional help will become a necessity. Should this be accomplished by bringing an aide or more help into the home, or should the patient relocate to a place where such assistance is provided (such as a senior residence, assisted-living residence, or a nursing home)? Home attendants should be carefully vetted, as they will be caring for a helpless and vulnerable individual. Agencies or case managers are valuable in vetting aides and home attendants. Should the patient relocate to be closer to family? Maintaining a sense of dignity and independence for the patient is paramount, and the family is usually at a loss of how to keep their loved one safe and avoid a fight, embarrass, or humiliate the patient.

Most institutions provide various levels of care and allocate sections of the facility for each level of care needed. Patients needing rehabilitative care are housed near each other. Those with incontinence or dementia in another area, etc. If the resident's needs change, they will be moved to another location in the facility. Some facilities are luxurious, with beautiful gardens, multiple dining areas, regular entertainment, libraries, clubs, art studios, and more. Some require purchasing apartments or homes in the facility with the rights of sale in the future. Some senior living facilities are located on college grounds and come with the opportunity to audit college-level courses at the school. There is much to choose from, and visiting a variety of facilities and collecting information is both instructive and valuable in helping to make the choice. As with anyone choosing where to live, there are no guarantees, and people often make decisions they later regret.

It's helpful to ask any facility what their policy is regarding residents wishing to move away or breaking a lease.

Private corporations may prefer people live at home, where no insurance payments would be needed. But few private insurance companies pay for institutional care. If institutionalized, most people will apply for Medicaid, a government insurance, to subsidize their care.

Chapter 9
STRUGGLING WITH END-OF-LIFE DECISIONS

A profound choice for patients, but rarely heeded by the disease

We each hope to have a long and comfortable life, including time to plan for when we become unable to manage our own affairs. Similar to planning for emergencies, people must think about advanced directives. But unlike unexpected emergencies, if lucky, we have lots of time to think about getting older and becoming less functional. We are not rushed into thinking about our choices. Nonetheless, even with a lifetime to prepare, a crisis usually happens, and plans must be made suddenly and without preparation. This can occur after an accident, a stroke, or the loss of a supportive care partner. As with disability or life insurance, we may wish never to need them, but it is prudent to have contingency plans regarding how we may wish to live or die. Surprisingly, even recognizing this, most people have never made these decisions known to their families.

With serious illness, patients or their families should anticipate that a medical team at a medical facility will present them with a series of questions and choices regarding end-of-life care. "Who is the patient's designated spokesperson, or health proxy, who holds the medical power of attorney (MPOA)?" This should be in writing. To avoid family disputes, all family members should agree with the choice. The health proxy should know the patient's preferences and must speak with the patient's voice and not give their own opinion. The medical POA is separate from the usual POA whose decisions concern property and assets. When the patient is unconscious or unable to express their preferences to their care providers, the medical proxy has to make the choices and give permission for all measures performed on the patient. If there is no proxy available, doctors will make the decisions in an emergency, or a temporary proxy will be chosen by hospital administrators.

The patient (or medical proxy) will be questioned about their choices regarding DNR (Do Not Resuscitate) and DNI (Do Not Intubate). Resuscitation is an attempt to restore a beating heart and functioning lungs to someone who has just expired. The objective is to reverse death, not prolong life. If the death is the culmination of a chronic disease, resuscitation is usually futile or very short-lived. There was a cause for the death, which was not corrected. If the death is from an acute event in an otherwise healthy individual, resuscitative measures will probably have more success. Another document that could be helpful is a Living Will. In this document, the individual outlines the conditions under which they would want care and those in which they would not. This anticipates the need for intubation (a breathing tube), tube feeding, or other life-maintaining measures. In the living will, they can stipulate a time dependency, such as allowing life-sustaining measures for a short period to test if they would be effective. If not effective at the end of a specified time, the patient requests they be terminated. These are very emotional decisions that usually cause stress and uncertainty. If unprepared, the respondent will be hesitant and anxious because of the life-or-death consequences. Too often, the person agreeing with the proposed plan of care begins to question their decision after several hours, discusses this with other family members, and spreads their anxiety throughout their circle of close contacts. It is usually not a question demanding an immediate response. The patient or proxy can ask for time to "think about it." It is also helpful to have other family members be aware of the choices and understand this is your decision. The consequence of not following this recommendation is having this choice become a trigger for family conflict and blame. These decisions can be changed or revoked at any time. They are not written in stone. However, at the time of a crisis, patients, if able, will make their own spur-of-the-moment decision, overriding anything they had previously expressed. This decision often is not the same as the one they made when feeling well and reflective. It is made when in pain or in distress. But this is the one the doctors will obey, nullifying any well-thought-out decisions of the family.

If conditions worsen, and the disease burden or breakdown of many organs and functions is too overwhelming to sustain life, the patient enters into a phase of dying. Doctors may recognize this (and patients may, too), but families frequently do not. Organ collapse and failure happens mostly in the most severely ill patients being cared for in Intensive Care Units (ICUs). Not accepting the death of their loved one, families may ask for "everything be done" to sustain life. Alternatively, doctors may suggest "palliative care." This form of care is aimed at providing comfort measures only and not treating the underlying disease, which doctors believe is no longer reversible. The goal is to allow the person to die in peace, without pain, and with dignity, avoiding the trauma of resuscitation, which would be futile in any event. In any case, the doctor should provide information to support reasonable expectations in the family.

News media sometimes publicize an extraordinary case of an individual for whom all expectation for survival had vanished, and doctors had felt the situation hopeless but who miraculously recovered and survived. This type of story gives renewed hope for miracles to happen. It supports desperate families of patients who are in the process of dying. They hope that if the patient is kept alive indefinitely, a miracle may happen, and their loved one will recover. There is a difference between living and merely existing; the former implies some hope for an iota of human cognitive activity. However, if there is no hope for recovery of a meaningful life, what is being accomplished by keeping a body alive by extraordinary measures? Would the affected patient want to exist in a vegetative state or perpetual coma? Furthermore, miracles are not the norm, and hoping for the one-in-a-million event to happen is wishful and fantasy thinking. In a hospital, other patients need the care and services of the staff whose attention is being focused on the dying patient. Is death just being postponed a few hours or days, and can aggressive therapy be justified? The hospital staff will try to be realistic, but also supportive.

Another choice for the patient or family is a request for hospice care. Hospices are a valuable resource for quality end-of-life care. Hospice care is a free service and can be offered to patients with a limited life expectancy (usually anticipated to be six months or less). This is relevant to patients with terminal diseases such as advanced malignancies or dementia, where there is no expectation of reversing the condition. Hospice care can be delivered in the patient's home or in hospitals. As with palliative care, hospice care is aimed at comfort care only, not managing the primary untreatable disease. Hospices generally have staff personnel available to assist the patient with help at all times, 24 hours a day, including nights, holidays, and weekends. They are staffed with well-qualified nurses to manage pain and give emotional support. They can assist in obtaining any equipment or supplies the patient needs. Hospices are authorized to give pain medicine and other drugs that many doctors feel uncomfortable prescribing. Nurses and therapists come to the home on regular visits to assess the home situation. Having hospice care available can be very reassuring to a terminally ill patient.

Considering end-of-life choices is a bit like considering life insurance - it's emotionally uncomfortable, and we would rather be thinking about more pleasant things. But know it is important, and that any or all advance directives can be changed or rescinded. Ambivalence is common, and older patients frequently change their minds about what they would or would not prefer. But it is their choice, and they should not be cajoled into choosing what the doctor or staff recommends. They and their family need to understand, in the most objective way, what choices are available. They may want to ask more questions and consult their clergy or other people they trust. The most important point is for the entire family to recognize and accept the wishes of the dying patient. If not, lingering accusations, blame, and antipathy can permanently disrupt family harmony. Despite the seriousness of these decisions, nature has a way of taking charge and making all the advanced planning irrelevant.

Chapter 10
CHOICES IN PREVENTIVE CARE AND EARLY DETECTION

An ounce of prevention is worth a ton of suffering

Preventive Care

Who can question whether preventing a problem is not far better for everyone than dealing with it? In Medicine, however, the term "preventive" is actually inappropriate; In medical care, "preventive" is only a relative term. There is no absolute prevention; only some reduction in risk acquisition and some degree of protection against severe disease. Few disorders have a single cause (such as in a sudden train wreck). The more contributing factors are known, the more targets are available for mitigation. This is good. Most of the more feared disorders have multiple risk factors that contribute to the final risk. Some risk factors are well understood, others strongly suspected, and still others only imagined. Mitigation of any of these risk factors may reduce final risk. These factors include genetic makeup and susceptibility (nothing we can do about this now). Lifestyle (this can be altered but will take great determination). Age, other illnesses or co-morbidities, and past illnesses (little we can do about this). Environmental exposures, toxic exposures, diet, immunizations, and medications (these are the most easily modified). But even small reductions in risk or acquiring some protection is better than none.

Corporations generally like preventive care, and support alternative and homeopathic care. From their perspective, such patient care is far less expensive than advanced specialty care. Prevention saves money, and alternative or homneopathic care generally does not require expensive testing and procedures. If their subscribers are happy with less expensive care, corporations will be more than satisfied.

The conditions we fear most and which can be partly prevented are osteoporosis and hip fractures, hardening of the arteries with subsequent strokes, heart attacks, poor circulation to the legs and kidneys, infections, some cancers, depression, some retardation of memory loss, loss of teeth, and pressure ulcers.

OSTEOPOROSIS: The single most common and feared event in an older patient is a sudden fall and hip fracture. It happens in an instant, unexpectedly, and can have catastrophic consequences. There is immediate pain and immobility, followed by hospitalization and surgery, followed by rehabilitation and slow recovery. Frequent complications include infections, blood clots, heart dysrhythmias, and even death. In a moment, the patient's life changes to one of being helpless, in pain, and vulnerable to many unpleasant events. It is not a quick event that is over in a moment. Everyone is at risk, and family life is changed.

The risk for a fracture (hip, pelvis, or spine) is dependent on the strength of the bone and the stress applied to it. Anyone who is hit by a truck, in a car crash, or falls out of the window will fracture even the strongest bones. Athletes in contact sports do this frequently without any signs of osteoporosis. Measuring bone strength would require increasing the stress on the bone to determine the amount at which it snaps. This cannot be done in living people. We use bone density scans as a poor but convenient substitute. As the name states, it measures bone density (the amount of material or mass in a given volume), not bone strength. Dense bones occur with some disorders. The bones are brittle and bleed easily. They are not strong.

Bone densities can be misleading. In cases of hip or spinal arthritis, calcium is laid down in the inflamed areas. Bone density will show greater density in these damaged sites, but these areas are not strong; they are arthritic or chronically inflamed. As with other testing methods, repeat bone density testing allows comparisons and assessments of how rapidly an individual is losing bone mass. Bone densities in one area are not indicative of the densities in another location. Generally densities are measured in both hips, spine, and pelvis. Obviously, if a density scan shows no calcium, there cannot be much bone, and the area will be weakened and vulnerable to breakage.

Bones are living tissue continually being remodeled, with absorption of older bone and the formation of newer. In childhood, bone formation exceeds bone resorption, and bones grow. With aging, bone formation slows, and reabsorption continues, leading to age-related bone loss. Menopause, with the change in hormones, brings accelerated bone loss for about a decade. Diminished bone mass is called osteopenia, while significant bone loss is osteoporosis. To understand the difference between strength and mass, consider two identical sheds being built. In the first, steel, wood, or cement supports are placed to buttress the walls and roof as directed by an architect. In the second hut, the same amounts of steel, wood, and cement are just piled on the floor. The two sheds will have identical densities but much different degrees of strength to withstand a storm.

To strengthen bone, calcium and bone formation have to be directed to the place of bone weakness and deposited in a precise way. With any structural support being modified, mechanical engineers or architects have to tell the builders where to place the supports. This is true as well with bones. The internal structure of the bone and the location of its calcium is not random. Its strength and resistance to fracture are determined by precise factors. If the individual has normal calcium levels, taking additional calcium does not direct it to be deposited where you want it to go. The individual runs the risk of depositing excess calcium into forming a kidney stone or increasing calcification of joints, arteries, and brain. If the patient is lucky, excess calcium will just be voided out in urine without doing harm. There is only one way to get the bone to ask for strengthening. That is weight-bearing exercise. The stress on our bones is our natural mechanical engineer and architect. Just walking puts stress on the hips and back, and specific points of stress will "ask" for strengthening. Having a limb in a cast for weeks will produce localized osteoporosis in the affected bones, which will resolve after the cast is removed and the limb is used. Astronauts must exercise while in space, or their bones will weaken considerably. Weight-bearing exercise is the prevention and will strengthen bones and muscles.

In addition to strengthening the bones, the risk of hip fractures can be reduced by reducing the risk of falling. Since most people spend the greatest amount of time in their homes, the home is the most common place for falling (the second most common area is at the street corner). A fall is most likely to occur in the bedroom or bathroom en-route to the toilet at night. It is then when it is dark and the person may still be half asleep and dizzy from suddenly standing; they may also be in a hurry because of urinary urgency. The pathway can be cluttered with shoes, disrobed clothing, or electric wires that create obstacles. And, if the individual had taken sleeping pills, it's even more hazardous. Falls can also be reduced by repairing loose door saddles, adding anti-skid pads to bathtubs or showers, laying down area rugs and bath mats, improving lighting, and installing grab bars along walkways and bathrooms near toilets, showers, and tubs.

Older people cannot recover from a loss of balance as quickly as can younger people. Reaction time is slowed. Consequently, when an older person loses their balance and begins to fall, they will. Patients can reduce falls caused by poor vision and balance with visits to the eye doctor and physical therapy including balance exercises and muscle strengthening programs.

Other measures to reduce accidents and fractures include installing corner protectors on any furniture along the walking path to cover sharp corners with soft padding. Stumbling against a pointed corner of furniture can easily cause a rib fracture. Hip protectors are inserts slid into specially designed undergarments that cushion the hip region from some stress with the fall.

Wearing appropriate shoes with good soles for traction can reduce falls out of doors. Using canes, walking poles, or walkers adds support and balance, takes the pressure off a painful leg, and is an effective way to reduce falling. If an individual needs assistive devices for walking safely and securely, they should use them. Vanity should never override common sense and safety.

But despite our best intentions and precautions, we all are at risk falling the "wrong way" and breaking our bones.

HARDENING OF THE ARTERIES: We recognize four major risk factors for developing advanced atherosclerosis: elevated blood pressure, diabetes mellitus, smoking, and elevated concentrations of Low-Density Lipoprotein cholesterol (LDL). Additional risk factors include genetic predisposition (family history) and elevation of some other blood components. The four major risk factors can be mitigated with medications, dietary changes, and counseling about lifestyle and habits. The more risk factors a patient demonstrates, the more aggressive they should be in managing each. The risk factors do not just pile up and add to the risk; they multiply and greatly increase risk.

Still, as we age, our arteries stiffen and become older. That's nature. We cannot retain the circulation of our youth through any known maneuvers. We hope our large arteries will age slowly and do not occlude in critical locations.

Occlusion of arteries can also occur due to emboli (clots or cholesterol plaques that break off a valve or artery and circulate until they get stuck), at which time they can occlude the vessel. Clots can form where blood stagnates, as in a fibrillating heart chamber. Circulation can also be lost when a blood vessel bursts (as with an aneurysm).

Taking a low-dose aspirin, an anticoagulant, a lipid-lowering drug, and controlling high blood pressure are all measures that can mitigate a stroke or heart attack.

INFECTIONS: Nature provides us with a good immune system to recognize and combat "foreign" substances. Stimulation of this system requires exposure to such substances, following which immunity develops over the weeks after exposure. Immune responses are directed at relatively small determinants of a complex organism like a virus or bacterium. An FDA (Federal Drug Authority) approved vaccine is one where the manufacturer has provided sufficient data showing adequate efficacy and safety. There are vaccines on the market directed against poisons or toxins (such as tetanus toxoid), bacteria (such as pneumococcal bacteria), and viruses (such as measles, mumps, and chicken pox). There is no vaccine that is 100% effective. Their efficacy is measured both by the levels of protection against acquiring the infection as well as how severe the infection would be. Protection is at both levels. The individual's immune response to any particular inciting agent (immunogen) is determined by the person's genetic makeup, their status at the time of immunization, the medicines they are taking at the time of immunization, and many recognized disorders that affect the function of the immune system. Consequently, the same vaccination may result in vastly different degrees of protection in different people.

Many individuals are afraid of vaccination, fearing the injection of foreign materials into their bodies, allergic reactions (which may be directed at materials other than the target immunogen), and doubting the vaccine efficacy after knowing an individual who contracted the disease for which they were vaccinated. This can occur when that individual makes a poor response to the vaccine, or the infecting agent does not have the precise antigenic makeup targeted by the vaccine. This latter event frequently happens with Influenza virus vaccines, developed against viral strains that are expected to be prevalent many months in the future. If a different strain appears, vaccination may be ineffective, as the immunity developed is directed against a different virus. There are potential side effects of vaccination that are uncommon but real and publicized by legitimate authorities. Still, often, people are afraid of immunization due to conspiracy theories and disproven data (the anti-vaxxers).

A new approach was developed with the COVID-19 virus immunization, and "vaccines" could be manufactured rapidly. With m-RNA vaccines (as with Covid), rather than injecting the foreign material to which we want the recipient to respond, the m-RNA vaccines contain the orders for the injected person to make the "foreign" proteins that, in turn, will stimulate the immune response.

The alternative to immunization, which will offer some protection to the infecting agent, is to avoid getting exposed: living in an isolated location, wearing effective face masks, gowns, gloves, and shields, or depending on luck and prayer. Herd immunity relies on others around you being vaccinated and protected against a particular infection. If they are protected, the unimmunized person has less chance of being exposed and infected.

DEPRESSION AND MEMORY LOSS: Actually, these two features can be linked, and there is a common entity called pseudodementia in people who are depressed. They manifest their depression with behavioral and memory changes simulating dementia. Depression is one of the most common and poorly diagnosed entities that injure the patient and the patient's family. It robs the affected individual of the ability to enjoy life and can devastate the entire family. Prevention of depression and memory loss usually requires outside assistance: social engagements, the need to address daily challenges, and a robust support system from friends and family. Other means include medication and counseling with professionals (clerical and secular) which can help in its management and prevention.

CANCER: Cancer is not one disease and behaves differently in different people. Some cancers can be prevented when we know the primary cause. However, the cause of many cancers has not yet been determined. For most lung cancers, the chief culprit is smoking, and smoking cessation can reduce the risk of getting lung, bladder, and kidney cancer. Many viruses can cause cancer in animals, and we now have a vaccine directed at the Human papillomavirus (HPV), which can cause cervical, penile, and skin cancers. Chemicals, such as asbestos and radiation exposures, are well documented to be carcinogens, as demonstrated with waters contaminated by fluorocarbons while making Teflon. Some Pesticides are carcinogenic, with more and more newly recognized environmental poisons having such a potential. To "prevent" cancers, people should be wary of exposure to complex chemical compounds that have not been adequately investigated for their safety. The dumping of wastes into runoff water and burning chemicals (as in military burn pits or the 9/11 burning at the World Trade Center, NY) exposes many to such dangers. Excessive sun and UV light exposure is associated with several types of skin cancer.

It is difficult to determine the association of any chemical with cancer. We cannot use people as test animals; it may take decades to see the connection, and there are so many different chemicals in our environment to which people are exposed that it may be hard to ascribe blame to any one agent. If laboratory testing of carcinogens in animals suggests an association, it is not proof that it will do the same in humans.

Most cancers are believed to have a multifactorial cause. There is no one thing to blame, but rather many conditions that bring on the cancer, such as multiple mutations or defects in a person's defenses. A strong argument can be made that finding cancer in a patient indicates the individual's immune system or body defenses were impaired. This theory claims we all develop cancers throughout our lives, but in the majority of cases, our defenses eradicate the cancer before it becomes an issue. It is a rare cancer that evades body surveillance and removal. It is doubtful we will ever be able to prevent all cancers.

DENTAL HYGIENE: As we age, bone loss affects the bones of the mouth and can loosen our teeth. Dentin and enamel are decreased. As a result, teeth loosen and can be lost, and many elderly people have difficulty chewing and eating a pleasing diet. Water fluoridation and better dental care and surveillance have limited the need for dentures, but patients must continually monitor their oral health with regular dental visits. Dental infections are common and can spread to other sites, with dire outcomes.

PRESSURE ULCERS: Here is a condition we really can prevent. When pressure is applied to an area of skin where there is little cushioning from fat or muscle over a bony prominence, we squeeze out the blood flow to the skin. The skin is being pressed against hard bone. Within two hours of blood deprivation, we can see microscopic damage to the skin. Watching people sitting or lying down, they will turn and readjust their positions regularly as the affected area causes them some discomfort. The ulcers can become large and infected, needing surgery and a great deal of effort to cure. Prevention is the answer. When people are immobilized by anesthesia, restraints, or paralysis, they must be passively turned or moved (even if just for a moment) to allow return of blood to the area. Alternatively, the pressure or weight must be distributed over a large area, not a pinpoint. Cushions, padding, bedding all can spread the weight and prevent sores. Pressure sores are evidence that the individual was unable to shift their weight or turn, either by themselves or by others.

Early Detection of Diseases

Even if not preventable, finding some diseases in their early stage (before they advance or spread) can be life-saving. Early detection is recommended for such disorders as colon cancer, prostate cancer, breast cancer, and skin cancer. Screening techniques include looking for blood or specific cancer-associated markers in the blood or feces, colonoscopies, regular pelvic exams, mammograms, EKGs, skin checks, chest x-rays, urine, and general blood test screens. For high-risk individuals, CT scans or MRIs can be ordered.

Most people recognize the value of early detection and request that all screening measures be done. A normal result is reassuring to them. But what, exactly, is the patient asking? Cancers can develop in any organ. So, are we planning to examine every organ for the presence of any cancer cells? Realize also that cells are microscopic. How many cells must be in a cluster to be detectable with the most sensitive scanning techniques available? A cluster of fewer than 1 million cells would be missed. Looking for the "footprint" (abnormal molecular products of the cancer also have thresholds for detection). Then, we also have the issue of determining when to begin the screening and when to stop. How often should the person be screened? A negative screening today does not mean it will remain negative in a month or a year. Recommendations are generally suggested by the appropriate medical society or “experts” who evaluate the literature and experience of doctors caring for these disorders and the use of common sense.

Screening for conditions not seen before a certain age makes no sense in individuals below that age. For example, there is no need to screen asymptomatic prepubescent girls or boys for pelvic, breast, or prostate cancer. We don’t start screening for colon cancer in normal individuals until the age of 45. For some other disorders, where life expectancy **with** the disorder far exceeds the life expectancy for an individual **without** that disorder, screening is not recommended. This holds true for prostate, pelvic, and breast cancer screening. When the individual’s life expectancy is less than ten years, and when these cancers are unlikely to cause death for more than ten years, should the test be done? Logically, there is no need to screen a 90-year-old woman for breast cancer. Since life expectancy now for men is in the early 80s and women in the late 80s (females generally live longer than their male counterparts in every mammalian species studied), should we stop screening for prostate cancer in men who are in their early 70s and breast or pelvic cancer in women who are in their late 70’s? These may be recommendations, but patients usually express their expectation to live well into their 90’s. This becomes a judgment call for the doctor and patient to make. Insurance carriers may have a different calculus.

How often should the screening be scheduled? Slow-growing cancers can be screened less frequently than fast-growers. Decreasing the screening interval from every ten years to every two years increases the cost 5-fold. This pertains to large populations since screening is for everyone, not just those with symptoms or signs of disease. It's a 5-fold increase for hundreds of millions of people. Some anxious people, or those with strong family occurrence of disease, may request and deserve screening more frequently. There has to be an element of reasonableness in this. We cannot screen twice a year, monthly, or weekly with tests that are expensive, laborious, or risky. It would bankrupt the economy, exhaust human resources, could cause more harm than value, and would be wasteful and probably useless.

We also do not look for blood markers of tumors and gene abnormalities that portend an increased risk of acquiring cancer (such as the BRCA gene) for screening purposes in the average individual. Family history is very relevant in making these determinations. These expensive screening tests are presently reserved for those only in the high-risk category or for following the progression of the disease or efficacy of treatment.

Chapter 11
CARE OF THE DISABLED

Those in need of the most medical care are often given the least

I can think of no group more negatively impacted by corporatized, regulated medicine than are the disabled.

As a group, the disabled comprise an increasing population, whose numbers have grown with the extended life afforded by advances in medicine and social programs. They are a very diverse population, encompassing individuals with birth defects and disabilities, those suffering from the consequences of accidents during their lives, those with chronic debilitating diseases and disorders, and those who, with advanced age, have lost their ability to function independently.

Physical disabilities include the loss of vision, hearing, speech, use of limbs, severe arthritis, neurological disorders, strokes, chronic pain, and mental changes and illnesses. The older diabetic patient may have all of the above. The result is a population who are not as functional nor as manageable as is the general population. They need special care and attention, which was more available in the personalized medical care of the past. Regulated, corporatized medicine does not currently allow for the time and individual attention these individuals require.

Furthermore, disabilities often multiply and increase the need for more medical attention: disabilities breed more disabilities. Immobility often leads to pressure ulcers and leg edema. The risk of aspiration and pneumonia are greater in those individuals who eat and drink while reclining or lying in a bed. Immobility increases obesity, decreased stamina, cardiopulmonary function, greater osteoporosis, and constipation. And immobility often leads to depression, which in turn can lead to greater immobility. Poor vision, hearing, and imbalance increase the risk of accidents, falls and fractures. The more disorders a person has, the greater the likelihood of their needing more medicines with an increased risk of developing adverse reactions to medications.

As we age, we all can expect to acquire some degree of disability. Disability comes in all degrees of severity and functional impairment. But all disabled patients need more attention and individual management than do normally functional patients.

Our bodies are made to be active and functional (at least until nature no longer needs us to procreate). And, aside from their disability, disabled individuals are, if not more, vulnerable to all the other afflictions humans can acquire.

Most disabled persons do not want to be a burden to their family or friends. They may try to do more than they are capable of doing. Other disabled individuals may feel they are worthless and withdraw into their own world. Some may be embarrassed and even apologize for their disability, as if it was their fault.

They do not currently receive the same medical attention that non- disabled individuals enjoy. Some of this is due to their feeling that their presence at the medical facility presents an imposition on the functioning of the facility by virtue of their need for greater time and attention. Most doctor's offices are not adequately equipped for dealing with the disabled. A doctor cannot examine a patient in a wheelchair or on a stretcher as well as patients on a modern examining table. And the disabled patient may not be able to change positions or perform a task requested by the examiner. The examining room may be too small to accommodate wheel chairs, walkers, scooters, or stretchers. Undressing or putting on an examining gown can be an ordeal for the disabled. As they know, a scheduled fifteen minute office visit is inappropriate to address all their medical and social concerns. They may require more than fifteen minutes just to be ready for the examination. They usually need the assistance of a family member or attendant to provide physical aid, and help with their history and recollections.

The look of despair or horror on the faces of office staff that they frequently encounter as they enter the office tells them their visit is not usually welcomed. Their health insurance may not provide the medical facility with adequate additional funding for their prolonged visit. To the doctor and the office staff, their visit will slow the office flow considerably in their patient schedules. Other patients in the waiting area recognize this, and may regard the presence of a disabled patient in the waiting area as a signal of a probable significant delay to their own visit and day's plans.

Consequently, many disabled individuals hesitate making a medical appointment when such a visit would be appropriate. "It is too much trouble, and the visit is usually too superficial," can be their reasoning. Indeed, just going to the appointment can be a hardship. It is far easier to remain at home and hope their condition will not worsen.

And, as discussed above, managed, corporatized medicine diminishes the unique aspects of the individual for the benefit of expediency and profit. Both of which suffer in caring for the disabled patient. As a result, disabled individuals, who usually require greater, more thoughtful, and personalized medical and social care, are short-changed in the world of corporate-controlled healthcare.

Most disabled individuals end up getting their care at public facilities: city, county, or state-operated outpatient clinics. These facilities are operated at public expense and are not profit-driven as are "private" facilities. Hours of operation are fixed and all staff are salaried for their services, with income not determined by the numbers of patients seen. Public facilities are another form of corporate managed-care, where the professionals are employees. In a way, this mimics the private, equity-owned facilities. They differ significantly, however, in the motives of the owners and who does the managing.

Chapter 12
PROTECTING YOUR HUMANITY

The public can influence the future direction of US healthcare

As previously stated, computers treat diseases, not patients. Doctors should treat patients, not diseases. This distinction is critical to maintaining our humanity. To paraphrase Dorothy in The Wizard of Oz, "We're not in the world of medicine that was practiced fifty years ago." The corporatization of medicine, algorithms, and artificial intelligence has changed everything. Computers and science have brought remarkable advances in medical care, but at a price. However, the practice of medicine possesses an art that cannot be programmed into a computer. The art of medicine concerns the human interaction between doctor and patient. This art is primarily inherent, learned, and copied. It is difficult to teach empathy or compassion to a computer or to those who lack these qualities. These are human qualities that bind people together. Computers don't care about humans and can't care for patients.

More and more, the doctor's time and effort is spent working (and sometimes fighting) with computers and EHRs. When patients complain about their health care, they list the same failings. "My doctor spent more time interacting with his computer than with me! I don't think I ever saw my doctor's face. I only saw the back of his head! My doctor never talked to me! My doctor never answers my phone calls! My doctor always seems to be rushing me out of the office! My doctor doesn't seem interested in me as a person! My doctor keeps sending me to different doctors for each complaint I mention and sends me for more expensive tests, which require a co-pay! My doctor just keeps writing prescriptions for more expensive pills! My doctor is never available - he or she always seems to be on vacation or out of town! My doctor seems more interested in making money than helping me!"

When we examine this list of complaints about their doctor, we are struck by the realization that these were the very same qualities and services that had been provided by the family doctor years ago: the family physician who cared for the patient as if they were a family member.

Dealing with insurance companies, testing facilities, and doctor's offices often leaves the patient upset and frustrated. The patient is an item in the computer program and is made to feel that way. Patients should not be talking back or disrupting the system. Computers function best when they interact with other computers. They deal in bites and numbers, not language and complaints. The corporate world of medicine thrives with computers. Time is money in the corporate world, and computers accomplish many tasks in much less time than people would. Furthermore, they don't get sick and require fewer benefits.

In dealing with the complex megastructure of the medical world, being hospitalized or referred to a large modern medical facility with many employees, impressive-sounding names, and imposing equipment in different facility locations, the patient may quickly feel overwhelmed, helpless, diminished, and dehumanized. Being in a foreign and frightening environment makes the patient feel even more insecure and vulnerable. But these feelings are unwarranted. As stated earlier, this needs to be corrected. All the structures, people, and machines are there for the patient's benefit. The patient is the reason for the very existence of this industry and its complexity. The patient is not the pawn but the boss, in a way. The patient's (and other patients') money pays for all this. Patients should assert their status and feelings without being overly bossy or demanding if they choose to be treated as human beings.

With advances in AI, we anticipate the development of more advanced computers and robots that will replace humans in many functions. Although advanced AI robots may be able to treat other AI robots and diseases for medical purposes, they will never be able to treat patients humanely. No matter how advanced, a robot can never have all the qualities of a person and will never be able to replace a human doctor caring for a patient. If you want your doctor to treat you as a person, the doctor must get to know you. It requires a greater awareness of your human qualities and needs. This information cannot be obtained from books, computer programs, or short patient notes. It evolves with time spent together and the doctor's recognition of the need to understand who you are.

As people become infirm or elderly, many become apologetic for their loss of independence and weakened status. Most are embarrassed to seek help and resent becoming a burden to their family, friends, or strangers on the street. Being sick or incapacitated is nothing to be ashamed of. It happens to everyone. It's not a badge of honor or something to be proud of either. It's a natural state and a natural occurrence. To most of your family or friends, your debility is their opportunity to show their love and care for you. It's their present to you, and you should accept it graciously, in the same way it was given. In the hospital or health center, the same rules apply, but for the staff, assistance is their job. You can be appreciative of their doing their jobs approvingly, but you don't need to apologize for your condition. You paid for their assistance, and you deserve it. It's a symbol of a shared humanity.

To maintain one's humanity when infirmed, debilitated, or aged, one must retain the essentials of being human. Humans are social beings and need social interactions with others. Isolation is not healthy for our psyche. We seek the company of others. Depression is common as people lose their prior capabilities. Depression robs the person of their most valuable possession - the ability to enjoy life. Being socially active helps fight depression. Individuals should keep their brains stimulated with continued learning and addressing challenges as best as possible. There are courses and lectures to take or attend at local schools, online, or libraries that cover all subjects. Acquiring hobbies such as painting, music, bonsai home planting, or reading keeps the person more involved in life. Volunteering in the community, schools, church, charity, or any activity gets the individual more engaged and motivated. It gives them purpose and reward. It may also help many others and reward the individual with a feeling of having value. Getting a pet provides company and, if a dog, a need for walking. The pet also returns your love. Some exercise and stretching are always recommended to keep the individual more flexible and energetic. The bottom line is to keep living and doing something. That is essential for maintaining your humanity.

Being alone and frightened in a foreign medical environment, the individual patient may easily feel overwhelmed. They have no trusted family doctor to comfort and guide them. They may sense that it is them against the medical bureaucracy. However, it should not feel like a "me vs. them" experience. Everyone involved in their care desires to restore their health and make them well again. It is not a "me vs. them" contest. It is an "us" allied against a disorder. That's what brings health and humanity together.

Medical care has transformed in the past several decades, as promoted by corporations and not challenged by the public. Medical care can be broken down into the What?, Why?, and the

Who? "What" refers to the complaint. What is the patient complaining about, the symptoms? The "Why" refers to understanding the disease. Why is this happening? What are the symptoms telling us? The "Who" is the individual, the patient, with all their human qualities.

As noted, the corporatization of medicine has essentially removed the "Who" for convenience and practicality. It diminishes the importance of an individual's characteristics. We are now witnessing a diminution of the "Why." In many places, medicine now focuses on the complaint, the "What." This makes medical care much simpler, faster, and cheaper. Treating the complaint directly addresses the patient's concerns on the most superficial level.

Such a progression to focusing on the complaint has its appeal. There is an infection - prescribe antibiotics. There is pain - prescribe anti-inflammatories or analgesics. Place a bandage over an injury. The patient's natural healing capacity should be able to handle the rest. Doctors will no longer be needed for the majority of patients' needs. The human side of medicine will be lost.

Getting rid of the "Who" is essentially endorsing a system that says, "Forget the patient, focus on the disease!" Getting rid of the "Why" changes this to, "Forget the disease, focus on the complaint!" This becomes the medicine of "Star Trek" as practiced by "Bones," the doctor. "Bones" was the starship "Enterprise" doctor, only because he had a useful hand-held device. He portrayed some compassion for the patient but dealt directly with the complaint. His device was the actual doctor, and it evaluated the "What." Anyone would have been able to use his medical device as effectively as "Bones." Bones did not need any special training besides using the hand-held device. While a grief superficial evaluation performed during a medical visit may be adequate for the majority of cases, many times the patient needs more human understanding and personal attention.

Unless the public objects to this dispassionate care, it may become the norm here on Earth. Doctors will become little more than technicians. If the public wishes medical care to refocus on treating a patient as a person and understanding the disease, there must be a concerted effort to change the trajectory of medical care. And since medicine goes where the money flows, and the public funds the entire industry, the public can exert its influence and show its wishes by favoring those systems and corporations that demonstrate their interest in preserving humanity - supporting organizations that fight for human values - and expressing their feelings to their government representatives. There is ample room in healthcare to accommodate human needs without restricting medical progress.

And since the caregiver-patient relationship is not one-sided, those directly providing medical care must also recognize the humanity of the patient. The caregivers are also human and suffer from burnout, frustration, and anger at how corporations deal with them. Many have lost their idealism and desire to help humanity, which they once displayed when entering their professions. Their independence and capacity to control their profession have been stolen. Corporatization of healthcare has certainly changed healthcare delivery, but it also impacts the motivation of prospective providers. What was the appeal of a healthcare profession career? What was the allure: Saving lives, working with people, a comfortable lifestyle, professional autonomy, continued intellectual stimulation and learning, job security, professional pride, helping others and feeling their gratitude, the challenge of dealing with real-life mysteries, the high esteem of the professions? The majority of these attractants have been eroded with the corporatization of healthcare. What will the next generation of doctors be like? What will appeal to them? Like patients, many doctors have bought into the corporate, regulated healthcare system we are entering and have lost the enthusiasm for healthcare they once had. They are acquiring a business perspective and shedding their professional one. With changing management and corporatization of healthcare, corporate executives' motivation has replaced caregiver's motivation.

Working in the corporate world, the power and allure of money may prove stronger than their interest in patient care. Corporations may merge and create larger conglomerates that dominate all aspects of healthcare. As with other industries, the specter of monopolies, driving out competitors, and the need for antitrust actions may extend to the healthcare universe. The patient has, or will feel the difference. Corporate management of industries is standard; they are businesses. In healthcare, however, such a business model is problematic. Here, we are dealing with a population who is generally older, sicker, more disabled, frightened, and vulnerable than average. They need more help, reassurance, support, explanations, and assistance to deal with their conditions. These are qualities of caring people who work with them, not those usually associated with corporate business managers. Who could have thought that healthcare, a service industry run and staffed by professionals, would be corporatized and dragged into the profit-motivated business world? It seemed too individual and personal to be computerized; too many uncertainties and human vagaries. Healthcare has existed since the earliest of times, and ideally, was always motivated by well-being and not by profit. Those who entered the profession professed their love for its mission and felt a need to help others. But now, in only a few decades, corporations and businessmen have found a way to take over this service and superimpose their profit mission.

Nonetheless, since healthcare will always revolve around the patient and their doctor or care provider (even with AI), there is an opportunity for change and reform in how medical care is delivered. Regardless of how healthcare is managed or funded, the delivery of the best available healthcare to the patient should be maintained. Patients should feel secure in their healthcare and health insurance and not be worried about coverage after the fact. The ultimate authority for changing and simplifying our healthcare system remains with the people, not the bureaucracies. Corporations can compete and challenge each other in terms of management but should not interfere with fundamental doctor/patient relationships. The involved parties should be put back into their appropriate roles. Insurance companies should stick to their objective of insuring and not directing health care. Health networks should advertise their differences and let the public choose which if any, network to join at their discretion and convenience (not when a window is open). This should be offered without jeopardizing their health insurance coverage. The government should set guidelines but not dictate medical care. Each component of the healthcare system should confine their activities to what they were trained to perform. Allow doctors to doctor. Medical decisions should revert to the doctor and patient alone, one human interacting with another human.

However, it is hard to slow or stop progress. Throughout the world, medical care will continue to become more corporate, managed, and less personal. That is the trend. In most advanced countries, national taxes support a national health system where the government pays for costs, and a managed care system operates. Those unhappy with this system can choose a more personal-care system with private health providers who are not paid from taxes. Choosing the private health system would require purchasing private health insurance. This creates a two-tiered system which is well tolerated and accepted. This may become the future of

American medicine if it is not blocked by our current corporations and elected officials, who now consider the development of national healthcare a form of socialism and a threat to capitalism. But even without a significant change in our healthcare system, I suspect there will always be isolated caregivers who will practice more personalized care. If the public supports these caregivers, their numbers may grow, and their presence will impact private and public corporation policies.

With the increasing corporatization of healthcare, patient choices will be reduced. The federal Medicare program is already being eroded by privatization with Medicare Advantage. The specter of corporate mergers, and having only a few healthcare conglomerates or syndicates controlling all American healthcare is frightening. The political power of such syndicates would rival the strongest lobbies in their influence on government. Consumer choices regarding doctors, facilities, laboratories, et al. will be limited and controlled by these healthcare syndicates.

So, what can be done if this scenario is unacceptable? As mentioned in Chapter 1, the doctor and the patient are at the center of the entire health industry, but have the least influence and say in its management. As individuals, their voice is weak and their power virtually nonexistent. Neither patients nor doctors are satisfied with how our healthcare is currently managed. Doctors are choosing to drop out of health networks or insurance plans, or become concierge doctors. Will healthcare continue to be attractive as a career choice? As for patients, they are powerless if acting alone.

Most Americans feel our healthcare system is far too complicated. It is fragmented with many disparate parties having different interests competing and interacting. With layers upon layers of regulations, bureaucratic policies, varying motives and goals, the consumer is rightly confused. For the average patient who only wants to be given healthcare for themselves and their families for whatever health needs arise, they are required to make critical choices from a vast assortment of policies covering the unexpected. Unlike fire, home, car, or life insurance, where the maximal insurance payouts can be determined, health insurance has no set limit. Medical and supportive needs and costs are impossible to predict, and costs of future therapies and treatments cannot even be imagined. How can any insurance company compose appropriate insurance costs for the unknown? This is true for both public and private health insurance. So private carriers throw the issue to the consumer who must choose the policy with what limits they can accept. The system needs to be simplified. Insurance companies know what is needed and can work together to offer only a few choices of policy.

Physicians and all caregivers have always valued their independence. For most physicians, the thought of being regulated by any outside organization was anathema. So how can doctors or patients influence the behavior of larger insurance or medical corporations? Complaints to elected officials rarely have an impact. Letters to insurance carriers do nothing. Ranting in the public square accomplishes nothing constructive. Alone, as individuals, people's voices are not heard. But their numbers are massive, and if organized, they can have a very loud voice.

Doctor's Council is a union that did a lot for its members, and their story can be a blueprint for future actions. The formation of the Doctor's Council succeeded in organizing physicians and Dentists working for the New York City or State Departments of Health into a labor union in the 1970s. Physician/labor organizers argued that there was no organized agency to represent state government medical employees, and as a consequence, NY state union law allowed this union to be formed. And why did the doctors employed by the city at city hospitals join the union? There was no choice. It was thrust upon them Only a few physicians and dentists advocated for creating the Doctor's Council to state authorities. They never even approached nor consulted the doctors they included in their union. There was an initial resentment of this surprising new entity, particularly since the union arranged to have its dues deducted from the salaries of physicians. However, the union quickly negotiated greater benefits, higher salaries, and better working conditions for the doctors and consequently gained broad support for the union. The union proved effective and beneficial to its members, even its retired members. Can this be copied nationally? Organizing doctors at large might be considered similar to herding cats. Still, if doctors nationwide could become organized or united into a single political and labor force, they would have a much stronger voice in determining the direction of medical care. There had been other mostly unsuccessful prior attempts to unionize doctors. An inherent problem (as with the police, fire, and other essential services) is that doctors cannot go on strike in good conscience. Their sworn oaths and commitments to their patients make going on strike anathema. They cannot endanger their patients. Nonetheless, doctors could demonstrate their value and exert pressure on their administrators by means of job actions: delaying or refusing to sign the forms required for payment of services. As the licensed professional needed to approve all documents regarding patient admissions, discharges, ordering testing or choice of medications, recommendations to patients of where to go for consultations, therapy, medications, etc., doctors can easily convince their network employers of their critical and valuable role in patient care. Many actions can be done that will not threaten patient safety and care, by which physicians can put tremendous financial and political pressure on insurance companies and health facilities. Organizing into a union with its unified, strong voice gives them much more clout, power, and influence than complaining as individuals. Unlike the AMA or other professional organizations, which focus on national health and the image of the profession as a whole, a union is focused exclusively on the welfare and benefits of its members. Other professional health providers may similarly unionize and gain greater power and influence. If organized and working together, health providers can change the status quo.

The public, too, must organize to acquire a greater voice and influence. Organizations can be supported that promote patient benefits. The important thing is to make noise and be noticed. Be noticed by politicians and by those corporations which are still competing for subscribers. By their taxes, insurance premiums, and payments for services, patients pay all the bills.

With cooperative effort by practicing physicians, patients, nurses, mental health providers, and therapists, a more satisfactory and compassionate form of medical care might be envisioned and achieved. It will require developing a revised healthcare system where all parties feel they are being treated and compensated fairly and appropriately. This will counter the dissatisfaction with medical care we now experience and reverse this trend of deprofessionalizing health professionals and regulating medical care by insurance companies.

Competing public and private healthcare systems may be needed to provide choices for consumers and to apply pressure on healthcare services to maintain a competitive high quality of care. Healthcare oversight currently lags behind corporatization. It is long overdue to create a National Health Authority or Board that can protect the public, set standards, and regulate the health industry with minimal political involvement or outside influence and interference. They can ensure that the American patient will continue to have choices in their healthcare and not be manipulated by syndicates motivated by profit.

Healthcare is changing. The time for the public to express its concerns is now. Healthcare is at a transitional crossroads. It needs oversight and concerned public pressure to curb corporate greed from dictating our health.

ACKNOWLEDGEMENTS

I want to thank my children: Drs. Donna Finkelstein, Steven Finkelstein, and Deborah Finkelstein for their valuable suggestions and insight needed for this book. Also very helpful were their spouses: Drs. Adam Ozols and Carole Hazan. Their complaints and suggestions were helpful. My brother, Dr. Solon Finkelstein shared many of his medical experiences with me.

Similarly, much of what I have learned about medicine has come from my personal family of physicians and health providers as well as colleagues.

And most importantly, I have learned much from my patients, friends, and peers who have shared their stories and complaints with me.

And in writing this book, I express my appreciation to Nada Glick and Marylyn Piven who advised and counseled me along the way.

ABOUT THE AUTHOR

Dr. Martin Finkelstein is a recently retired board-certified internist and geriatrician. For over fifty years, he practiced medicine and geriatrics in New York, NY. He was a clinical associate professor of medicine at NYU-Langone Medical Center in NYC, where for many years he participated in the teaching and training of medical students, junior faculty, colleagues, and nursing students, as well as learning from his patients.

Dr. Finkelstein graduated from New York University School of Medicine with Honors in Microbiology and received his postgraduate training in Internal Medicine at NYU and Bellevue Hospitals in New York and Stanford-Palo Alto Medical Center in Palo Alto, California, where he completed a fellowship in Infectious Disease. Dr. Finkelstein was a flight surgeon in the US Air Force. He had extensive experience in conducting medical and basic science research, teaching medicine and geriatrics, and patient care. Dr. Finkelstein has traveled extensively around the world and has observed the practice of medicine in many different communities.

Dr. Finkelstein was repeatedly cited in Castle Connelly's "America's Top Doctors" and in New York Magazine's "Best Doctors in New York" in the area of geriatrics.

Dr. Finkelstein comes from a family of doctors in which more than a score of family members are, or were, physicians - most of whom graduated from NYU School of Medicine. Dr. Finkelstein grew up in a home where his father, an internist and family physician, had his office. His three children are practicing physicians in the NY metropolitan area, two of whom are married to practicing physicians. Dr. Finkelstein thus has a rare personal view of medicine as it was practiced and how it has changed over the past 75 years. Looking back at how the practice of medicine has changed, Dr. Finkelstein considers himself a *medicosaurus.*

The impetus for writing this book is his awareness of current public discontent and ignorance about medical care and medicine as a profession and as it is now managed. The paradigm of how medicine should be practiced is not what it had been. Circumstances have changed, and this book speaks to the changes; pros and cons.

Other books by Dr. Finkelstein

Finkelstein Martin, *Aging, Health Care, and You: A Doctor's Personal Prescription for Understanding and Improving Your Health Care. Lessons, Insight, and Informative Practical Guidance for the Aging Health Care Consumer*. 2012.

Finkelstein Martin, *Adam's Creation. Eden at Falls-speak. A Center for Tolerance, Respect, and Understanding.* (a novel), 2019.

Finkelstein Martin, *What You Should Have Learned on Earth.* (a novel), 2022.

www.ingramcontent.com/pod-product-compliance
Lightning Source LLC
LaVergne TN
LVHW022043200926
848481LV00003B/771
* 9 7 9 8 3 4 8 5 7 2 2 9 7 *